Social and Emotional Learning Interventions

Under the Every Student Succeeds Act

EVIDENCE REVIEW

Sean Grant, Laura S. Hamilton, Stephani L. Wrabel, Celia J. Gomez, Anamarie Whitaker, Jennifer T. Leschitz, Fatih Unlu, Emilio R. Chavez-Herrerias, Garrett Baker, Mark Barrett, Mark Harris, Alyssa Ramos

RAND CORPORATION

Commissioned by

The Wallace Foundation

Supporting ideas.
Sharing solutions.
Expanding opportunities.

For more information on this publication, visit www.rand.org/t/RR2133

Published by the RAND Corporation, Santa Monica, Calif.

Cover: Martin Barraud/Getty Images

Preface

The reauthorization of the U.S. Elementary and Secondary Education Act, referred to as the Every Student Succeeds Act (ESSA), emphasizes evidence-based interventions while giving states and districts new flexibility on the use of federal funds, including funds that could be used to support social and emotional learning (SEL).

The RAND Corporation reviewed recent evidence on U.S.-based SEL interventions for K–12 students to better inform the use of SEL interventions under ESSA. This report discusses the opportunities for supporting SEL under ESSA, the standards of evidence under ESSA, and SEL interventions that should be eligible for federal funds through ESSA. Federal, state, and district education policymakers can use this report to identify relevant, evidence-based SEL interventions that meet their local needs.

This research was conducted in RAND Education (a division of the RAND Corporation) and commissioned by The Wallace Foundation. The Wallace Foundation is committed to supporting programs and practices that help children and young people develop the social and emotional skills they need for success, and to commissioning research that contributes credible, useful evidence to the field.

Contents

Figures and Tables

Figures

Tables

Summary

Among educators and researchers, there is growing acknowledgement that student success depends not only on achievement in core academic subjects but also on learning a broader range of intrapersonal and interpersonal competencies. Efforts to develop these competencies are often described using the phrase *social and emotional learning* (SEL). Although the federal Every Student Succeeds Act (ESSA) legislation does not explicitly mention SEL, educators and policymakers can leverage funding offered under ESSA to support evidence-based programming that is related to SEL and that meets the legislation's requirements (Public Law 114-95, 2015).

To help decisionmakers understand how ESSA addresses SEL and to provide guidance regarding SEL interventions that will satisfy the ESSA evidence requirements, we examined recent peer-reviewed research evaluating the effects of SEL interventions in U.S.-based, K–12 public schools.

ESSA Supports for SEL

ESSA contains both direct and indirect opportunities to support SEL. To take advantage of these opportunities, educators need to understand how to leverage the law's funding streams. Title IV (21st Century Schools), which authorizes spending between 2017 and 2020 for programs aimed at improving educational opportunities, provides the most directly relevant funding stream for SEL. In addition, Titles I (Improving the Academic Achievement of the Disadvantaged) and

II (Preparing, Training, and Recruiting High-Quality Teachers, Principals, or Other School Leaders) provide opportunities to support SEL. Other sources of funds that focus on specific subpopulations might also be appropriate for SEL interventions. For example, states can prioritize SEL in their ESSA plans by including SEL measures in their accountability outcomes. However, the future of the policies around ESSA, funding allocations discussed below, and the resulting implementation of the law are subject to change. Consequently, state and local education agencies should continue to monitor communications from the U.S. Department of Education for up-to-date information regarding ESSA.

Defining *Evidence* Under ESSA

ESSA requires the use of *evidence-based* interventions for a number of funding streams. The legislation defines three levels, or *tiers*, of evidence from empirical research: strong (Tier I), moderate (Tier II), and promising (Tier III) evidence. ESSA also includes an additional level (Tier IV) that does not require existing empirical evidence but instead requires (1) that the intervention is supported by a strong rationale for believing the intervention is likely to improve the targeted outcomes and (2) that an evaluation of the intervention is under way. Because of vagueness in the legislation, the U.S. Department of Education developed nonregulatory guidance that recommends additional, more-detailed criteria for identifying evidence at each of the four tiers. However, the nonregulatory guidance is just that—suggested but not required—and it is not mentioned in the legislation itself. Further, some ambiguity about ESSA evidence requirements still remains, enabling different interpretations and implementations of the evidence-based definitions provided in ESSA. Because our report aims to identify interventions that meet ESSA evidence tiers as they stand now, we do not apply criteria that are more detailed and stringent than those consistent with a reading of the ESSA statute and nonregulatory guidance. That said, we support future efforts to further clarify ESSA evidence requirements and explore more-stringent criteria for the highest tiers.

SEL Interventions with Tier I–III Evidence

We identified 60 SEL interventions that meet the first three tiers of evidence under ESSA (Tiers I–III) from evaluations that took place in U.S.-based, K–12 public schools. Across the entire body of evidence, educators have options of SEL interventions that have positive results on intrapersonal and interpersonal competencies, academic attainment and achievement, disciplinary outcomes, civic attitudes and behaviors, and school climate and safety. The majority of interventions have been validated at the elementary school level and in urban communities, although numerous interventions have positive results at other school levels and in other communities. A significant number of interventions have been validated with samples of students who come from low-income families or from racial or ethnic minority groups. Furthermore, many evaluations reported professional development of and implementation support for intervention providers, and several interventions have a dedicated website.

Guidance for Tier IV Interventions

While this review focuses on SEL interventions with Tier I–III evidence, Tier IV offers educators the flexibility to implement interventions that lack empirical research yet meet local needs. The requirement to evaluate Tier IV interventions is an important tool to continue to build the evidence base for SEL interventions and thereby expand the range of interventions available to future educators. Numerous free, online resources discussing the development of logic models and the design of evaluations are available for educators interested in implementing Tier IV interventions (see Chapter Six for examples). To promote greater chances for success, local education agencies should consider partnering together in their efforts to experiment with new interventions and rigorously evaluate their results.

Looking Ahead

Key Findings

- ESSA supports SEL through several different funding streams.
- We identified 60 SEL interventions that meet ESSA evidence requirements.
- Educators in elementary schools and urban communities have the most options for SEL interventions that meet ESSA evidence requirements.
- Interpersonal competencies are the most common outcomes with positive results in studies of evidence-based interventions.

Recommendations

- Use this review to find SEL interventions meeting ESSA evidence Tiers I–III.
- Take advantage of Tier IV flexibility for interventions with no empirical research.
- Address local conditions to facilitate effective intervention implementation.
- Look beyond explicit interventions when designing approaches to promote SEL.
- Provide professional development and other supports to build educators' capacity to gather and use evidence.
- Continue to improve SEL measurement.
- Provide feedback on remaining ambiguities of evidence tier requirements.

Acknowledgments

We are grateful to the staff of The Wallace Foundation who provided invaluable input throughout the project and on this report. Specifically, we appreciate the probing questions from Wallace Foundation staff during a briefing on key findings, and we especially appreciate the ongoing support of Hilary Rhodes. Kathryn Young, Catherine Holahan, and Scott Palmer of Education Counsel provided legislative analysis of ESSA, and their suggestions markedly improved the quality of the report. Brittany Seymour provided excellent administrative support on all aspects of the project. We also thank Becki Herman and Brian Stecher from the RAND Corporation; Stephanie Jones from the Harvard Graduate School of Education; Sandra Wilson from Abt Associates; and Roger Weissberg from the Collaborative for Academic, Social, and Emotional Learning for feedback on our thinking throughout the project. Jody Larkin from the RAND Knowledge Services department ably carried out a massive literature search, and her knowledge and experience were essential for helping us refine the search and review process. Finally, we are grateful to Catherine Augustine and Jill Cannon from RAND and to Sandra Wilson from Abt Associates for their thoughtful reviews of this report, and to Phyllis Gilmore from RAND, who edited the final version. We take full responsibility for any errors.

CHAPTER ONE

Introduction

The Every Student Succeeds Act (ESSA) legislation (Public Law 114-95, 2015), which reauthorized the Elementary and Secondary Education Act, emphasizes the need for schools to adopt activities, strategies, and interventions (collectively referred to as *interventions*) that are supported by research evidence when using federal funds. The law's emphasis on evidence reflects broader trends in federal and state policymaking to gather and use high-quality research to inform decision-making. The growing availability of resources, such as the What Works Clearinghouse (WWC), supports the efforts of educators and policymakers to consider whether an intervention in question is likely to produce the outcomes they desire (Institute of Education Sciences [IES], undated c). Given the wide range of interventions that are available to schools, and the massive amount of unfiltered information educators receive about interventions from vendors and other sources, consolidated resources that facilitate evidence-informed decisions are especially valuable.

A growing body of research suggests that, to be successful, students not only need to master core academic subjects, such as mathematics and reading, but also need to demonstrate competency in a wide variety of cognitive, affective, and behavioral domains. Although much of the policy discussions surrounding ESSA and school improvement have focused on academic skills, the legislation addresses a broad range of school-improvement efforts and student outcomes. One particular set of outcomes that has been of increasing interest to education stakeholders in recent years is the broader range of intrapersonal and interpersonal competencies that help students succeed both in and out of school. These competencies are sometimes described as "social and emotional" competencies or skills, and the development of these competencies is often described using the phrase *social and emotional learning* (SEL). The ESSA legislation does not include "social and emotional" but does include several provisions that are relevant to SEL, as we discuss later in this report. When policymakers and educators are thinking about evidence-based programming that will meet the requirements of ESSA, they might want to consider interventions that are designed to promote social and emotional competencies as part of their overall improvement strategy.

The primary goals of this report are to help decisionmakers understand (1) how ESSA addresses schools' efforts to promote students' social and emotional competencies and (2) which SEL interventions meet ESSA evidence requirements. Our review focuses on interventions that have an explicit primary aim of improving students' social and emotional competencies and are delivered to universal populations of students in school settings (see discussion of the various approaches to SEL later). The primary audiences for this report include policymakers and practitioners who are responsible for setting policies or selecting programming for schools. The report may also be of interest to out-of-school-time providers; several of the interventions that we review involve an out-of-school-time component. Although other reviews of SEL interventions have been published, this report uniquely reviews SEL interventions in the context of ESSA evidence tiers and the opportunities to use federal funds to support SEL. This report is the latest in a series of evidence reviews commissioned by The Wallace Foundation that provide guidance on evidence-based interventions under ESSA across various priority topics in education (Herman et al., 2017; Ludwig, Boyle, and Lindsay, 2017). This series complements other efforts to help educators understand and apply ESSA evidence requirements, including the "Evidence for ESSA" website developed by the Center for Research and Reform in Education at Johns Hopkins University (Center for Research and Reform in Education, 2017).

What Is Social and Emotional Learning?

In this report, we use *SEL* to describe efforts promoting a variety of competencies that research has shown to be important for student success in school and in life. These competencies are sometimes described using other labels, such as *character* or *noncognitive skills*; Lash and Belfiore (2017) provide a summary of various approaches to categorizing these competencies. Market research funded by The Wallace Foundation suggests that the phrase *social and emotional learning* is more likely than other phrases to be familiar to, and accepted by, practitioners, policymakers, and family members than other ways of describing these competencies (Loeb, Tipton, and Wagner, 2016).

A National Research Council (NRC) report summarized research on competencies that contribute to successful experiences in school, the workplace, and life more broadly, categorizing the competencies into three broad areas (NRC, 2012, p. 4):

- *Cognitive competencies* include mastery of academic content in such subjects as mathematics, science, language arts, foreign languages, history, and geography and of skills related to critical thinking, creativity, and argumentation.
- *Intrapersonal competencies* include attitudes and behaviors, such as conscientiousness, initiative, flexibility, emotional regulation, and grit, which can influence how students apply themselves in school and in other settings.
- *Interpersonal competencies* include the skills needed to relate to other people, such as communication, collaboration, conflict resolution, and leadership.

It is important to note that including a category labeled *cognitive* could be misinterpreted as suggesting that the skills in the other categories do not draw on sophisticated mental activity, and many scholars have argued that this distinction should be avoided (see, e.g., Conley, 2013).

In this report, we focus on intrapersonal and interpersonal competencies, which capture the competencies that are most often described as part of SEL. Several other frameworks and approaches to categorizing these competencies have been published, and many of them are widely used by schools, after-school programs, and other entities. For example, the Collaborative for Academic, Social, and Emotional Learning (CASEL) has developed a commonly used framework that includes five dimensions (see box).

CASEL's self-awareness and self-management dimensions include competencies that would be categorized as "intrapersonal" in the NRC framework, while the CASEL social awareness and relationship

CASEL Core Competencies

Self-awareness: "The ability to accurately recognize one's own emotions, thoughts, and values and how they influence behavior. The ability to accurately assess one's strengths and limitations, with a well-grounded sense of confidence, optimism, and a 'growth mind-set.'"

Self-management: "The ability to successfully regulate one's emotions, thoughts, and behaviors in different situations—effectively managing stress, controlling impulses, and motivating oneself. The ability to set and work toward personal and academic goals."

Social awareness: "The ability to take the perspective of and empathize with others, including those from diverse backgrounds and cultures. The ability to understand social and ethical norms for behavior and to recognize family, school, and community resources and supports."

Relationship skills: "The ability to establish and maintain healthy and rewarding relationships with diverse individuals and groups. The ability to communicate clearly, listen well, cooperate with others, resist inappropriate social pressure, negotiate conflict constructively, and seek and offer help when needed."

Responsible decisionmaking: "The ability to make constructive choices about personal behavior and social interactions based on ethical standards, safety concerns, and social norms. The realistic evaluation of consequences of various actions, and a consideration of the well-being of oneself and others." (CASEL, 2016) skills dimensions fall into the NRC "interpersonal" category. CASEL's responsible decisionmaking dimension has aspects of both intrapersonal and interpersonal competencies. Additional ways of organizing and labeling social and emotional competencies include those developed by the University of Chicago Consortium on School Research (Farrington et al., 2012; Nagaoka et al., 2015), Stephanie Jones and colleagues (Jones and Bouffard, 2012; Jones, Brush, et al., 2017), the Forum for Youth Investment (Smith, McGovern, et al., 2016), and Transforming Education (2016). Despite the diversity of terms used to describe social and emotional competencies and the variety of approaches to categorizing them, the intrapersonal and interpersonal domains provide a substantively meaningful and intuitive way to categorize the social and emotional competencies that are addressed in research on SEL interventions. Therefore, we focus on that distinction throughout this report.

Efforts to address students' social and emotional competencies in schools can take several forms (Kendziora and Yoder, 2016). For example, a recent brief by CASEL (Dusenbury et al., 2015) describes four broad approaches to promoting SEL:

- explicit, freestanding SEL instruction that aims to develop specific competencies
- general teaching practices that support classroom environments characterized by shared expectations, positive relationships, and other features that promote SEL (e.g., use of group work to facilitate collaboration)
- integration of SEL instruction into the academic curriculum (e.g., engaging students in complex mathematics problem-solving activities to help promote persistence in addition to mathematics learning)
- efforts to create a schoolwide climate and conditions that foster SEL, including new disciplinary approaches and a common vision.

To keep the scope of our review manageable, the primary focus of our report is on the first of these approaches, although many interventions included in our review also involved one or more of the other approaches. Although explicit instruction is only one approach to promoting social and emotional competencies, focusing on explicit SEL instruction is potentially valuable because research suggests that many students enter school without having developed these competencies and could benefit from direct instruction to help develop them (Jones and Bouffard, 2012). Nevertheless, we encourage educators reading this report to consider all these approaches as they develop and implement strategies to improve SEL in their schools.

Why Should Schools Emphasize Social and Emotional Learning?

Schools throughout the United States are under tremendous pressure to produce high scores on academic achievement tests while also addressing a variety of other student needs and challenges. Given the many demands on teachers, principals, and other school staff, educators may also find an additional expectation to improve students' social and emotional competencies daunting. However, there are at least three reasons schools and educators should view SEL as a priority.

First, research suggests that an emphasis on SEL can enhance, rather than detract from, schools' core missions of promoting academic achievement and attainment (Osher et al., 2016). For example, a review of SEL interventions indicated that students who participated in these programs outperformed other students in several areas, including academic achievement (Durlak et al., 2011). A recent follow-up to this review found that these benefits persisted 6 to 18 months postintervention (Taylor et al., 2017).

Second, evidence suggests that explicit SEL interventions are effective in helping students develop social and emotional competencies and improve other aspects of students' lives above and beyond the effects of academic achievement. SEL interventions can improve students' attitudes toward themselves and others, social behaviors, and behavioral problems (Durlak et al., 2011; Jones, Brush, et al., 2017; Yeager, 2017). In addition, a substantial and growing body of research demonstrates the powerful relationships between social and emotional competencies and success in various contexts, including outcomes later in life, such as earnings and criminal activity. For overviews of this research, see NRC (2012) and National Academies of Sciences, Engineering, and Medicine (2016).

Finally, in recent years, most states have revised their academic standards or adopted new ones, including the Common Core State Standards and the Next Generation Science Standards.[1] These standards have broadened the range of competencies that students are expected to demonstrate—for example, by increasing the emphasis on communication, collaboration, and persistence. Several states have also adopted separate SEL standards (as of February 2017, 11 states had SEL standards for at least some grade levels in their K–12 systems), reinforcing the message to schools about the importance of promoting these competencies (CASEL, 2017). A related trend has occurred over the past several years in the area of assessment, where practitioners and researchers have been engaged in a research and development effort to create measures of social and emotional competencies (National Academies of Sciences, Engineering, and Medicine, 2016; Soland, Hamilton, and Stecher, 2013; Stecher and Hamilton, 2014). This growing emphasis on competencies beyond those associated with traditional academics is partly a response to calls by employers and institutions of higher education for raising student competencies and performance in domains related to SEL.

Taken together, these recent developments in policy and research suggest that students are likely to benefit when schools offer high-quality SEL interventions. Additional in-depth sources of information on evidence-based SEL interventions include the CASEL guides (CASEL, 2013; CASEL, 2015), *Navigating SEL from the Inside Out*, a report by Stephanie Jones and colleagues (Jones, Brush, et al., 2017), and the 2015 *Handbook of Social and Emotional Learning* (Durlak et al., 2015). Our report is unique in its focus on providing explicit guidance

---

[1] Although several states that originally adopted Common Core have formally withdrawn from that initiative, most of their standards are quite similar to Common Core. See, e.g., Korn, Gamboa, and Polikoff, 2016.

for the use of federal funds to promote SEL and classifying SEL interventions according to ESSA evidence tiers. In the next chapter, we discuss how ESSA offers several opportunities for federal funds to be used in ways to support school and district initiatives that focus on SEL.

Organization of This Report

We began this report by defining SEL and explaining why it should be a primary consideration for schools as they plan their curricula and instructional programming. We next describe how ESSA addresses SEL (Chapter Two) and how the law approaches evidence (Chapter Three) before moving on to describe the scope and methods of our review (Chapter Four) and the results of that review (Chapter Five). In Chapter Six, we provide guidance for readers who are interested in adopting interventions that do not meet ESSA standards for empirical evidence. We conclude the body of the report with a brief discussion of implications and recommendations in Chapter Seven. Appendix A expands on material in Chapter Four. Appendix B and a companion volume expand on material in Chapter Five.

CHAPTER TWO

How Does the Every Student Succeeds Act Support Social and Emotional Learning?

The ESSA legislation does not explicitly reference SEL.[1] However, ESSA policy provides opportunities to incorporate SEL interventions into the work of schools, districts, local education agencies (LEAs), and state education agencies (SEAs). The policy language includes calls for improving school conditions for student learning, enhancing peer interactions, providing a well-rounded education, and incorporating programs and activities that promote volunteerism, community involvement, or instructional practices for developing relationship-building skills.

Educators interested in incorporating SEL interventions into school practices have opportunities to support these efforts by leveraging federal funds ESSA authorizes. In this chapter, we present a brief overview of the specific funding streams within ESSA that may be used to support SEL interventions and initiatives. Title IV funds are the most directly relevant, but Titles I and II also provide opportunities to support SEL. In addition to the funding streams we describe in this chapter, other sources of federal funds that focus on specific populations exist that might be suitable for use in SEL instruction. States can prioritize SEL in their ESSA plans (e.g., including indicators related to school climate or student engagement that are related to social and emotional development as part of the Indicator of School Quality or

[1] We searched the policy language for terms often used to label social and emotional competencies. These included *character education*, *noncognitive skills*, and both *intrapersonal* and *interpersonal skills*. There are no explicit references to these broad identifiers.

Student Success in a statewide performance indicator system).[2] Open opportunities also exist for districts and schools to focus on SEL (e.g., communicating that SEL interventions may be part of Title I grants). Together, the ESSA funding streams that we discuss in this chapter enable educators not only to adopt the types of explicit SEL interventions that are the focus of this review but also to address SEL more broadly through other activities, such as integration of SEL into academic instruction or efforts to improve school climate and culture. However, the future of the policies around ESSA, the funding allocations discussed here, and the resulting implementation of the law are subject to change. SEAs and LEAs must continue to monitor communications from the U.S. Department of Education regarding ESSA to ensure all practices comply with the most recent regulations.

Title I: Improving the Academic Achievement of the Disadvantaged

Title I of the ESSA legislation authorizes approximately $62.5 billion of education spending between 2017 and 2020 in the form of formula grants to states.[3] This funding stream provides opportunities to incorporate SEL into school operations in three main ways: schoolwide programs, targeted assistance programs, and school supports and improvement activities.

A modest proportion of Title I funds go toward district and school development of schoolwide and targeted assistance programs

---

[2] Identifying appropriate measures or reviewing the evidence base on summative SEL measures that can be used in consequential accountability is beyond the scope of this work. Selecting such measures requires state policymakers to gather additional information about technical quality and understand that the specific method(s) of constructing an indicator may or may not be consistent with what evidence suggests (Chiefs for Change, 2016b). The Learning Policy Institute recommends that states not use measures of students' social and emotional competence, at least not in the short term (Melnick, Cook-Harvey, and Darling-Hammond, 2017). They argue that most SEL measures were not designed for cross-school comparisons and, thus, are not appropriate for consequential accountability.

[3] Actual funding appropriations may be lower than the authorized amounts identified in the legislation. This is true for all funding streams discussed in this report.

that support the progress of, in particular, low-income students toward meeting challenging academic standards (see "Schoolwide Programs" [Sec. 1114] and "Targeted Assistance Schools" [Sec. 1115] of the Elementary and Secondary Education Act as amended by ESSA). These funds can be used for both academic and nonacademic subject interventions. For example, the legislation requires schools to include a description of how the practices chosen will "use methods and instructional strategies that strengthen the academic program in the school, increase the amount and quality of learning time, and help provide an enriched and accelerated curriculum, which may include programs, activities, and courses necessary to provide a well-rounded education" (Sec. 1114(b)(7)(A)(ii)). Thus, a school may be able to incorporate in its plan SEL interventions that improve the quality of learning time through a reduction in classroom behavioral disruptions. Interventions used for schoolwide and targeted assistance programs do not need to meet a specific evidence threshold as defined by ESSA evidence standards (which we discuss further in Chapter Three and the remainder of the report).

Every state is required to set aside 7 percent of Title I allocations for school support and improvement activities in the schools the state identifies as the lowest performing each year (see Sec. 1111(d)(2) of ESSA). These funds are awarded on a formula or competitive basis to LEAs and must be used to support implementation of interventions and practices that improve student outcomes. These student outcomes could include social and emotional competencies if schools or districts (LEAs) can demonstrate a need; all school improvement plans for schools identified for comprehensive support and improvement must be informed, in part, by the indicators a state uses in its performance system and the results of a school-specific comprehensive needs assessment. For instance, a school could utilize measures of student discipline, absenteeism, student engagement, or school climate data in the needs assessment to identify for the school improvement plan a need for SEL interventions that would address areas of low performance. As another example, educators may also be able to incorporate SEL interventions in school improvement efforts if a needs assessment demonstrates that classroom peer collaboration would effectively improve

English and language arts outcomes. All school improvement plans that are being funded with federal funds must include at least one evidence-based intervention with at least strong, moderate, or promising evidence. These interventions must thus meet criteria for Tiers I through III, which require empirical evidence from intervention evaluations and are the focus of our review.

Title II: Preparing, Training, and Recruiting High-Quality Teachers, Principals, or Other School Leaders

The ESSA legislation authorizes approximately $11.1 billion in spending over four years (2017–2020) to support the preparation, training, and recruitment of educators at all levels of the school system. States could potentially use Title II, Part A formula funding to support educators in their capacity to provide instruction that promotes students' social and emotional competencies. Moreover, these funds may also be applicable to the development of school leaders and educators to *assess* social and emotional competencies, as well as to *implement* associated interventions. In addition to outlining specific allowable uses of funds focused on professional learning and educator preparation, recruitment, and retention, the Title II Part A formula program allows states and districts to support "other activities identified by the state" that meet Title II purposes. Most of these key allowable uses of funds must be evidence-based "to the extent the State determines that such evidence is reasonably available." This evidence must meet one of ESSA's four tiers.

Two competitive grants under Title II can be used to support SEL. States can apply for competitive Supporting Effective Educator Development grants (Title II, Sec. 2242) to provide evidence-based professional development for addressing the needs of LEAs and the students the LEAs serve. A Supporting Effective Educator Development grant could be used, for instance, to offer professional development that helps teachers implement instructional practices related to SEL. The School Leader Recruitment and Support Fund (Title II, Sec. 2243) is directed toward developing the capacity of school leaders to succeed in high-needs schools, with a priority on entities that will implement evidence-based activities within the top three tiers of evidence under ESSA. If, for example, a high-need school used Title I resources to support an SEL intervention, it might also use School Leader Recruitment and Support Funds to support related evidence-based professional development of school leaders for that same intervention.

Title IV: 21st Century Schools

ESSA Title IV authorizes more than $7.3 billion over four years to support a variety of programs aimed at improving the educational opportunities of students. Student Enrichment and Academic Support Grants require districts to allocate at least 20 percent of the grant funding to support the provision of a well-rounded education, at least 20 percent to support the development of safe and healthy students, and a portion of funds to support the effective use of technology. Districts receiving over $30,000 in grant funds must conduct comprehensive needs assessments that address each of these areas, and particular allowable uses of funds require evidence to support them (e.g., discipline practices) to the extent that the state determines such evidence is reasonably available.

Title IV monies also cover the provision of both academic and nonacademic supports explicitly outside of the regular school day. Such activities are covered through the allocation of separate formula grants to states (e.g., 21st Century Community Learning Centers). Additionally, competitive grant allocations in the Title IV funding stream support national programs that have an SEL component, such as Promise Neighborhoods and Full-Service Community Schools. Here, schools and local community organizations have the opportunity to identify a wide array of interventions that are aimed at improving the educational opportunities of students.

Summary

The language of ESSA provides ample opportunity for SEAs, LEAs, and schools to incorporate SEL initiatives into their efforts to support low-income students and enhance school improvement efforts. These initiatives include opportunities to prepare educators to deliver high-quality SEL instruction and assess the learning of students in domains related to SEL. Any selected intervention will need to meet a minimum standard of evidence, as defined by the particular section of the legislation where that use of funds is allowed or encouraged. In the next chapter, we discuss how ESSA defines its evidence tiers and summarize the associated guidance on the legislation.

Summary of Key ESSA Funding Streams That Can Support SEL Programming

Title I: Improving the Academic Achievement of the Disadvantaged

Part A: Improving Basic Programs Operated by the Local Education Agencies ($15 billion)

Schoolwide Programs[a]
Targeted Assistance Programs[a]
School Support and Improvement Activities[a]

Title II: Preparing, Training, and Recruiting High-Quality Teachers, Principals, or Other School Leaders

Part A: Supporting Effective Instruction

Formula Grants to States ($2.3 billion)[a]

Part B: National Activities

Supporting Effective Educator Development ($53 million)[b]
School Leader Recruitment and Support ($16 million)[b]

Title IV: 21st-Century Schools

Part A: Student Support and Academic Enrichment Grants ($1.65 billion)

Student Enrichment and Academic Support Grants[a]

Part B: 21st Century Community Learning Centers ($1 billion)

State Application[a]
Local Competitive Subgrant Program[b]

Part F: National Activities

Promise Neighborhoods ($72 million)[b]
Full-Service Community Schools ($10 million)[b]

NOTE: States and districts may identify additional ways to support SEL beyond the funding streams identified here. Moreover, actual funding appropriations may be lower than the authorized amounts identified in the legislation.
[a] Distributed through formula funds.
[b] Distributed through competitive grants.

CHAPTER THREE

How Does the Every Student Succeeds Act Define *Evidence*?

The ESSA legislation includes several provisions that require interventions to be supported by evidence when schools or LEAs use federal funds to pay for the interventions. The policy defines four levels, or *tiers*, of evidence that reflect varying degrees of methodological rigor (see box, p. 18).[1] ESSA legislation labels the first three tiers as *strong* (Tier I), *moderate* (Tier II), and *promising* (Tier III) evidence. The fourth tier (Tier IV) does not have an agreed-on label but has been called "demonstrating a rationale" (AEM Corporation, 2016; Herman et al., 2017), "research-based rationale" (Ludwig, Boyle, and Lindsay, 2017), "strong theory" (Chiefs for Change, 2016a), "evidence-building" (Results for America, 2017), or "under evaluation" (West, 2017). We use *demonstrating a rationale* to refer to Tier IV in the remainder of this report.

Tier I evidence must come from the most rigorous experimental design for causal inference—a randomized controlled trial (RCT). In an RCT, participants are randomly assigned to either receive the intervention or participate in a comparison group that does not receive the intervention. RCTs are often considered the gold standard for evaluating the effects of interventions (Torgerson and Torgerson, 2001). Tier II evidence must come from rigorous quasi-experimental research, which approximates experimental research by identifying a comparison

---

[1] The evidence tiers are described in detail in other literature reviews of arts education (Ludwig, Boyle, and Lindsay, 2017) and school leadership (Herman et al., 2017).

> **Definition of *Evidence-Based* in ESSA**
>
> In Title VIII, Sec. 8002(21)(A), ESSA defines *evidence-based* as
>
> an activity, strategy, or intervention that
>
> (i) demonstrates a statistically significant effect on improving student outcomes or other relevant outcomes based on—
>
> (I) **strong evidence** from at least 1 well-designed and well-implemented experimental study;
>
> (II) **moderate evidence** from at least 1 well-designed and well-implemented quasi-experimental study; or
>
> (III) **promising evidence** from at least 1 well-designed and well-implemented correlational study with statistical controls for selection bias; or
>
> (ii) (I) demonstrates a rationale based on high-quality research findings or positive evaluation that such activity, strategy, or intervention is likely to improve student outcomes or other relevant outcomes; and
>
> (II) includes ongoing efforts to examine the effects of such activity, strategy, or intervention.

group that is similar to the intervention group participants on observed preintervention characteristics (e.g., test scores). Tier III studies must include a comparison group that did not receive the intervention, yet comparison group participants are not as rigorously matched to intervention group participants as required for Tier II evidence. To address selection biases that may result, a key feature of Tier III evidence is that methodological or statistical techniques must be used to reduce or account for differences between the intervention and comparison groups, such as statistical controls for students' gender, race, prior test scores, or parent education level.

Tier IV differs substantively from Tiers I through III in that it does not involve direct empirical evidence on the relationship between intervention receipt and outcomes of interest. Instead, Tier IV is defined by two features. First, an intervention must be supported by a strong rationale connecting specific intervention components to the expected outcomes produced by the intervention. Second, there must be a current evaluation under way on this intervention. Because Tier IV does not require existing empirical evidence, a literature review that is designed to gather research-based evidence is not well-suited to identifying interventions that could potentially meet the Tier IV requirements. Therefore, our evidence review in Chapter Five focuses only on Tier I–III interventions, while Chapter Six provides a separate discussion of ways educators can meet Tier IV evidence requirements when implementing interventions that lack empirical research yet meet local needs.

The legislation determines which tiers of evidence must exist for certain allowable uses of each of the funding streams. The policy does not, however, determine the specific tier of evidence (of those permissible within a funding stream) that schools must utilize to inform intervention choices. In contrast, the nonregulatory guidance from the U.S. Department of Education on using evidence to strengthen education investments under ESSA (discussed in the next section) recommends the use of the highest tier of evidence available, ideally Tier I or II evidence. Finally, the policy allows flexibility in applying the evidence standards for Title II and Title IV funds. Specifically, it suggests that states (in consultation with LEAs in the state) determine whether the necessary evidence is "reasonably available" for identification or whether non–evidence-based interventions can be used in the absence of such reasonably available evidence.[2]

Nonregulatory Guidance on Evidence

Beyond defining what is meant by *evidence-based*, the legislation does not explain what qualifies as "well-designed" or "well-implemented" experimental (Tier I), quasi-experimental (Tier II), and correlational (Tier III) studies. For instance, there are no established rules for which

---

[2] Neither the legislation nor nonregulatory guidance define or clarify what "reasonably available" evidence means.

statistical controls are required to address selection bias,[3] and the legislation does not predetermine which "student outcomes or other relevant outcomes" must be measured for an intervention to be considered evidence-based. This ambiguity allows substantial room for SEAs or LEAs to interpret the evidence requirements in distinctly different ways.

Because of the ambiguity in the legislation's definition of what constitutes Tier I–IV evidence, the U.S. Department of Education issued nonregulatory guidance on September 16, 2016, to provide states with additional information on selecting and using evidence-based interventions under ESSA. By its nature, nonregulatory guidance does not mandate the information to be used (i.e., it is nonbinding) but is provided for "convenience and is included to offer examples of the many resources that educators, parents, advocates, administrators, and other concerned parties may find helpful and use at their discretion" (U.S. Department of Education, 2016, p. 2). Guidance also often serves as a set of "safe harbor" parameters for grantees as they interpret the law. Prior evidence reviews supported by The Wallace Foundation (Herman et al., 2017; Ludwig, Boyle and Lindsay, 2017), "Evidence for ESSA" (Center for Research and Reform in Education, 2017), and Results for America (undated) have all utilized this guidance in their work.

According to the guidance, well-implemented and well-designed Tier I studies should meet WWC evidence standards without reservations or be of similar quality for making causal inferences (i.e., would likely meet the WWC criteria but have not gone through a full WWC review). Tier II studies should meet the WWC evidence standards with reservations or be of similar quality. Rating studies as meeting WWC standards "without reservations" focuses on proper randomization and sample attrition, while rating studies as meeting WWC standards "with reservations" focuses on equivalence of the intervention and comparison group at baseline. In addition, WWC establishes require-

---

[3] Selection bias involves systematic differences between preintervention (i.e., baseline) characteristics of intervention and comparison group participants. The evidence tiers in ESSA are ranked according to their ability to address selection bias, with RCTs providing the strongest method for preventing systematic differences, on average, between intervention and comparison-group participants at baseline.

ments for outcomes and analyses for results within studies meeting WWC standards to be eligible for review. The general WWC evidence standards found within the *What Works Clearinghouse: Procedures and Standards Handbook* (IES, 2014) are then tailored for specific content area reviews, such as character education interventions (IES, 2006).

In addition to referring to WWC standards, the guidance explicates several additional criteria for Tiers I and II beyond what ESSA's definition requires. To satisfy Tier I or Tier II requirements, an intervention's evidence should

1. show a statistically significant and positive effect of the intervention on student outcomes or other relevant outcomes[4]
2. not be overridden by statistically significant and unfavorable effects from Tier I or Tier II studies[5]
3. be based on a large sample (at least 350 students) and conducted in multiple sites (at least two districts, LEAs, localities, or states)
4. be validated with a population (both the demographic sample and the setting for Tier I; either the demographic sample or the setting for Tier II) that reflects the population of students or schools set to receive the intervention.

The guidance provides little clarification for Tier III evidence; it states only that a well-designed and well-implemented correlational study uses sampling and/or analytic methods to reduce or account for differences between the intervention and comparison groups. The results of these evaluations, according to the guidance, must be statistically significant and favorable for the intervention and should not be overridden by statistically significant unfavorable evidence from Tier I or Tier II studies.

The guidance for Tier IV expands on the ESSA language by providing a few additional suggestions for demonstrating sufficient ratio-

---

[4] The nonregulatory guidance defines *relevant outcomes* as those the intervention is designed to improve.

[5] Essentially, policymakers are trying to prevent practitioners from using only positive findings to support the use of a preferred intervention and, instead, are requiring all relevant research on a particular intervention to be considered.

nale and ongoing research efforts. First, the guidance recommends having a "well-specified logic model that is informed by research" for Tier IV evidence (U.S. Department of Education, 2016, p. 9). Moreover, the ongoing research efforts should be designed to produce promising, moderate, or strong evidence. The guidance does clarify that a district interested in implementing a new intervention is not necessarily the party responsible for conducting an evaluation. For example, if a district in Nebraska is looking to use an intervention, and a district in Tennessee is conducting an evaluation of that same intervention, Nebraska could rely on the Tennessee district's evaluation to meet Tier IV requirements.

Table 3.1 summarizes the evidence requirements for each funding stream and provides examples of activities that schools could adopt using the funds. This list is not exhaustive but is intended to illustrate the variety of approaches to promoting SEL that can be funded under ESSA.

Eligible Outcomes

Both ESSA and the nonregulatory guidance provide for flexibility in the outcomes that evaluations have measured or will measure. A thorough reading of the ESSA legislation offers some insight into the types of outcomes policymakers took into consideration when prioritizing initiatives, funding opportunities, and state accountability systems (see box, p. 24). As mentioned in the previous section, intervention evaluations must demonstrate favorable effects on student achievement or other relevant outcomes, yet "other relevant outcomes" are only defined broadly as those outcomes a particular intervention is expected to change. Thus, for SEL interventions, evidence would likely need to be based on outcome measures for the specific social and emotional competencies that the intervention targets or on one of the many performance areas identified in the legislation (e.g., academic achievement, school safety).

Table 3.1
Opportunities for Funding, Evidence Required for Funding, and Eligible ESSA SEL-Related Activities, by ESSA Title

Opportunities for Federal Investment in SEL, by Title, in ESSA	Evidence Required for Funding	Examples of Potentially Relevant Activities (Funded by ESSA and Relevant to SEL)
Title I, Part A: Improving Basic Programs Operated by the Local Education Agencies	Tiers I, II, III, or IV allowable for a subset of Title I activities Tiers I, II, or III only required for at least one intervention in schools identified for comprehensive and targeted support	• Schoolwide or Targeted Assistance programs, including academic and nonacademic subject interventions to support the progress of students toward meeting challenging standards • School support and improvement activities focused on improving student outcomes in low-performing schools; can be used for SEL interventions if justified by a needs assessment
Title II	Tiers I, II, III, or IV Most allowable uses of funds must be evidence-based to the extent that the state finds that such evidence is reasonably available	• Professional development for teachers and school leaders, including for the provision of explicit SEL instruction and for integration of SEL into academic instruction
Title IV	Tiers I, II, III, or IV	• Student support and enrichment activities that promote social and emotional outcomes • Expanded learning time that addresses SEL • Efforts to promote safe and healthy schools through the provision of SEL instruction • Implementation of community schools that emphasize students' academic as well as nonacademic needs

ESSA Outcomes

The following potential student achievement and other relevant outcomes are referenced in ESSA:

1. academic achievement and closing achievement gaps
2. growth in academic achievement
3. English-language proficiency
4. graduation rates
5. student engagement
6. educator engagement
7. student access to and completion of advanced coursework
8. postsecondary readiness
9. school climate and safety
10. dropout prevention and/or reduction
11. school safety measures (suspensions, violence, arrests, referrals)
12. absenteeism (excused and unexcused)
13. discipline actions (disproportionate use of out-of-school/class sanctions)
14. college-going
15. workforce readiness
16. successful transitions from pre-K to kindergarten, to middle grades, and to high schools

Branded and Nonbranded Interventions

The ESSA legislation gives considerable flexibility to states and LEAs in deciding which "activity, strategy, or intervention" to implement, regardless of whether it is a branded or nonbranded intervention. *Branded* interventions are those that are created and sold by developers. These interventions are more likely to have name recognition, more-rigorous evaluations, and formal implementation support (Herman et al., 2017). *Nonbranded* interventions tend to be developed locally but may consist of activities or components similar to those in branded interventions. Both branded and nonbranded interventions may be supported by empirical evidence from an evaluation. States and LEAs are able to select an intervention so long as it meets one of the evidence tiers required for the particular funding stream. They might also choose to replicate the key features of a branded intervention while adapting other elements of that intervention to address local needs and priorities. According to personal communication between the authors of the prior RAND review of school leadership interventions and the U.S. Department of Education, "[t]he label or brand attached to a program or intervention included in a research study is less important than the activities, strategies, and practices that constitute that program or intervention" (see Herman et al., 2017). However, although the law indicates no preference or priority for either branded or nonbranded interventions, some branded programs might have a greater chance of replicability because they are documented in manuals and because dedicated purveyor organizations that assist in training and implementation are more readily available.

Summary

The ESSA legislation requires the use of evidence-based interventions for many of the education initiatives supported through federal funding. However, ESSA's description of the four evidence tiers is broad and ambiguous. The subsequent nonregulatory guidance defined *evidence-based* to help SEAs, LEAs, and schools apply the evidence-tier requirements. This guidance provided more detail on the quality or rigor of a research design expected for an empirical study to be classified as Tier I, II, III, or IV. However, the guidance is just that—suggested but not required—and it is not mentioned in the legislation itself. Further, some ambiguity remains, allowing different interpretations and implementations of the evidence-based definitions provided in ESSA. Because our review focused on identifying interventions that meet ESSA evidence tiers as they stand now, we did not apply criteria that are more detailed and stringent than those consistent with a reading of the ESSA statute and nonregulatory guidance. Finally, while the legislation permits both branded and nonbranded interventions, branded interventions are more likely to be the focus of empirical studies, to meet the higher evidence tiers (i.e., Tiers I–III), and have resources available to support implementation. In the next chapter, we discuss the scope and methods of our evidence review.

CHAPTER FOUR

Our Approach to Reviewing the Evidence on Social and Emotional Learning Interventions

Key Questions Guiding Our Approach

We examined recent peer-reviewed research literature to identify evidence on SEL interventions meeting ESSA's requirements. Two key questions guided our approach:

1. What SEL interventions have recently been evaluated in U.S.-based, K–12 public schools?
2. What SEL interventions have yielded evidence meeting ESSA Tiers I–III?

We summarize our approach in this chapter and provide further technical details in Appendix A.

Information Sources We Used for Our Literature Search

We conducted a comprehensive search of the major electronic databases of indexed scientific literature (the Education Resources Information Center [ERIC], Education Abstracts, PsycInfo, Scopus, and Web of Science) and relevant websites on SEL research to identify evaluation reports on SEL interventions. We limited our search to reports published from 2002, when the U.S. Department of Education's IES began substantial investment in rigorous education intervention research (Public Law 107-279, 2002), to September 2016. In collaboration with a reference librarian from RAND's Knowledge Services, we used the NRC (2012) framework to develop search strings for these databases using terms related to SEL, intervention research methods, U.S.-based schools, youth, and academic outcomes. We conducted both a broad search for SEL interventions generally and targeted searches for the branded SEL interventions we had identified through previous literature and correspondence with experts in the area. Our search focused only on full-text reports (conference abstracts were excluded) published in English. We removed any duplicates arising from the multiple searches.

Criteria We Used to Identify ESSA-Eligible Studies

We used the NRC SEL framework to develop inclusion and exclusion criteria to apply to retrieved literature according to the seven domains from Petticrew and Roberts (2008): participants, interventions, comparators, outcomes, timing, settings, and study design. (See Table 4.1 for details of our eligibility criteria.) Overall, we included studies on SEL interventions involving activities, techniques, or strategies in which social and emotional competencies (e.g., self-awareness, self-management, social awareness, relationship skills, and/or responsible decisionmaking) are taught to, modeled for, and/or practiced and applied by students (Durlak et al., 2011).

To determine whether studies constituted Tier I evidence, we examined whether they (1) randomly assigned participants (or groups of participants) to either the SEL intervention or a comparison group and (2) experienced low attrition using the liberal boundary from WWC's procedures and standards (IES, 2014). If an RCT had high attrition, we considered its eligibility for Tier II. We assessed studies' eligibility for Tier II by examining whether they established baseline equivalence between the groups in the analytic sample on either (1) a pretest in the same domain as the outcome or (2), if such a measure did not exist, on a measure of academic achievement and socioeconomic status (IES, 2016). If a study being assessed for Tier II did not demonstrate that groups in the analytic sample were equivalent at baseline, we

Table 4.1
Eligibility Criteria for Evidence Review

Domain	Criteria
Participants	• We included studies with samples of students in grades K–12. • We excluded studies with samples of pre-K youth, postsecondary youth, and youth not currently enrolled in school.
SEL interventions	• We included branded and nonbranded programs, policies, practices, and products that – have a primary aim of promoting SEL in the intrapersonal or interpersonal domains of the NRC framework – target a general population of students (as opposed to individual students or groups of students specifically selected or indicated for a given risk factor) – are delivered directly to students in classrooms or in a school setting. We considered out-of-school-time interventions delivered through a public school as eligible. • We excluded studies on the following: – unintended or unplanned actions and events that had an impact on SEL – interventions with the primary purpose of promoting motivation or achievement in specific academic disciplines (e.g., reading, math) – general classroom practices not intentionally seeking to improve social and emotional competencies – interventions focused on students' physical health and development (e.g., substance use, pregnancy, dating violence) – interventions not delivered to students directly (e.g., positive behavioral intervention support frameworks or professional development of school personnel) – interventions delivered only to special populations of students or specially assembled "at risk" groups of students.
Comparator interventions	• We excluded studies that involved only head-to-head comparisons of two SEL interventions.
Outcomes	• We included studies that examined at least one measure in the following domains: – intrapersonal competencies (i.e., mind-sets, knowledge, attitude, skills, and behavior related to self-awareness, self-management, and responsible decisionmaking about personal behavior) – interpersonal competencies (i.e., mind-sets, knowledge, attitude, skills, and behavior related to social awareness, relationship skills, and responsible decisionmaking about social interactions) – academic achievement (standardized assessments only) – academic attainment – disciplinary outcomes – civic attitudes and behaviors – school climate and safety.

Table 4.1—Continued

Domain	Criteria
	• We excluded outcome measures that had questionable reliability or validity for the intended purposes, were overaligned with the SEL intervention as defined by WWC Evidence Standards, or were not administered in a standardized manner for all participants.[a]
Timing	• We included studies of any intervention duration and follow-up period. • We included studies in which the intervention was delivered during the school year or though summer learning programs from 1994 to the present. • We included studies that were published in 2002 or after.
Setting	• We included studies conducted in public schools serving any grades K–12—including public charter, magnet, and alternative schools. • To identify evidence most applicable to ESSA, we excluded studies located outside of the United States, its territories, or tribal entities.[b] • We also excluded SEL interventions delivered solely online.
Study design	• We included evaluations of SEL interventions that had at least one analysis of an eligible outcome meeting ESSA Tier I, II, or III.

[a] A recent blog post by Slavin and Kim (2017) contains some recommendations for SEL measures that are more stringent than those found in the ESSA legislation and nonregulatory guidance (e.g., a focus on objective, observable measures that are verified independently). While there is reason to be concerned about the validity of some student and teacher self-report measures, as well as performance and detection biases, we retained any measures in our review if they were clearly not overaligned with the intervention, were administered in a standardized way, and had some evidence of validity and reliability, to be consistent with the nonregulatory guidance.

[b] U.S. territories and constituencies include the Bureau of Indian Education, Department of Defense Dependents' Schools, Department of Defense Education Activity, American Samoa, Guam, Northern Mariana Islands (also referred to as Northern Marianas), Puerto Rico, and the U.S. Virgin Islands.

considered its eligibility for Tier III. For Tier III, we examined whether studies assessed a statistical correlation between intervention assignment (SEL or comparator) and an eligible outcome, and included a methodological or statistical control for selection bias.

As discussed in previous chapters, our review did not include Tier IV studies. Instead, we have included guidance for educators to help document that an intervention that they want to implement but that has not yet been empirically evaluated meets Tier IV evidence requirements (see Chapter Six).

How We Selected Studies for Our Review

Two independent reviewers screened the title and abstract of each retrieved citation against our eligibility criteria. Next, we attempted to obtain full-text manuscripts to more fully assess the eligibility of each citation judged as potentially eligible by at least one reviewer during title and abstract screening. Two independent reviewers assessed these full texts for eligibility. We resolved disagreements between the two reviewers through a third reviewer and/or discussion within the review team.

How We Collected and Classified Information from Eligible Studies

Two independent reviewers extracted study-level information and outcome data from each eligible study (see Appendix A for a full list of the information we collected). Outcomes of interest included ones that align with the NRC framework's intrapersonal and interpersonal domains; standardized assessments of academic achievement in mathematics, English language arts, and reading; academic attainment; disciplinary outcomes; civic attitudes and behaviors; and school climate and safety. Two independent doctoral-level reviewers assessed the methodological quality of included studies according to ESSA standards and assigned each finding to an ESSA evidence tier:

- Tier I includes statistically significant, positive findings from studies that randomly assigned participants (or groups of participants) to the SEL intervention or comparison group and had low attrition.
  - Individual findings from a study that randomly assigned participants could be assigned to a lower ESSA evidence tier if the

analysis violated the randomization and/or attrition requirements.
  - An outcome could cumulatively meet the large sample (at least 350 students) and multisite (at least two districts, LEAs, localities, or states) sample requirements if multiple studies meeting the other Tier I requirements found a positive result for this outcome.
- Tier II includes statistically significant, positive findings from studies that established baseline equivalence between the groups in the analytic sample and either (a) nonrandomly assigned participants (or groups of participants) to the SEL intervention or comparison group, or (b) randomly assigned participants (or groups of participants) to SEL or comparator interventions but had *high* attrition (overall and/or differential).
  - Individual findings from a study with baseline equivalence could be assigned to a lower ESSA evidence tier if the analysis involved an analytic sample that did not establish baseline equivalence.
  - An outcome could cumulatively meet the large sample (at least 350 students) and multisite (at least two districts, LEAs, localities, or states) sample requirements if multiple studies meeting the other Tier II requirements found a positive result for this outcome.
- Tier III includes statistically significant, positive findings from studies comparing participants (or groups of participants) receiving an SEL intervention with a comparison group that failed to meet either Tier I or Tier II but methodologically or statistically controlled for potential confounding factors.
- If there was not conclusive evidence that a finding met an evidence tier, we assessed it at the next lowest tier.
  - Because we relied solely on the information reported in the manuscripts of identified studies, we noted any reasons for assigning a study to a lower ESSA evidence tier due to ambiguities in the study reports. Interested readers could submit a query to the authors of such a study for further information if

they would like to assess whether the study could meet a higher tier.
  - All interventions in our list of evidence-based interventions at least meet Tier III standards.
- For each relevant outcome meeting the standards for Tiers I–III, we assessed whether study findings were statistically significant and favoring the SEL intervention ("positive"), not statistically significant ("ns"), or statistically significant and favoring the comparator intervention ("negative").
  - In keeping with the nonregulatory guidance from the U.S. Department of Education, we used this information to exclude interventions from our list of "evidence-based" interventions if (1) all findings for eligible outcomes were not statistically significant or (2) at least one result was negative for an eligible outcome measure.
  - When included studies reported sufficient data, we also calculated effect sizes according to WWC procedures and standards for outcomes meeting Tier I or II (i.e., evidence suitable for making causal inferences). To be consistent with WWC evidence standards, we did not calculate effect sizes for outcomes meeting Tier III unless they were downgraded because of the sample size or multisite requirement from the nonregulatory guidance (which WWC does not enforce).
- In addition to assigning each study finding to an evidence tier, we also assigned each intervention to an evidence tier based on the highest rating achieved by any outcome across all studies.

It is important to note that our tier assignments—particularly assignments of Tier I or II—should *not* be considered official determinations that a study meets WWC standards (with or without reservations). Although our methods are based on WWC procedures and standards, our tier assignments may not map perfectly onto determinations about studies meeting WWC standards because of: discrepancies between the nonregulatory guidance and WWC procedures and standards in characterizing study findings, sample size requirements, and multisite requirements; missing information in manuscripts on included studies for which WWC would approach authors; and the ability for SEAs or LEAs to consider evidence "of similar quality" and therefore interpret ESSA evidence requirements in distinctly different ways.

In the next chapter, we summarize the results of our evidence review.

CHAPTER FIVE

Evidence-Based Social and Emotional Learning Interventions Under the Every Student Succeeds Act

In this chapter, we provide summaries across evidence-based SEL interventions under ESSA by outcomes, school levels, settings, samples, and intervention features. These syntheses aim to provide an overview of recent evaluations of universal, U.S.-based, SEL interventions for K–12 students. For those interested in intervention-specific information, we provide brief evidence tables at the end of this chapter summarizing each evidence-based intervention at each school level, a more detailed evidence table in Appendix B, and a more extensive overview on each intervention in a companion volume (Grant et al., 2017). Appendix B also includes recommendations on how educators can use these evidence tables and the more detailed information in our companion volume to select relevant, evidence-based interventions that best serve the needs identified by their needs assessments. The more detailed summaries for each evidence-based intervention in our companion volume also indicate whether the intervention was included in the CASEL guides (CASEL, 2013; CASEL, 2015) or in the Jones et al. (2017) review, for the benefit of interested readers.

Search Results

Our search identified more than 24,000 citations, of which 4,943 went through full-text eligibility assessment, yielding 150 manuscripts of eligible studies evaluating 68 branded and unbranded SEL interventions. Of these interventions, four had an evaluation in which the research design criteria for Tiers I–III were met, yet there were no statistically significant positive results on any of our outcomes of interest: Girls in the Game (Bohnert and Ward, 2013), Lessons in Character (Hanson et al., 2012), Peer Group Connection (Johnson, Simon, and Mun, 2014), and Teacher-Child Interaction Training (Fernandez et al., 2015). In addition, four interventions had an evaluation in which the research design criteria for Tiers I–III were met, and there was a statistically significant *negative* result on an outcome interest: Creating a Peaceful School Learning Environment (Fonagy et al., 2009), on a measure of school climate and safety; Guiding Responsibility and Expectations for Adolescents for Today and Tomorrow (Farrell, 2008), on a measure of interpersonal competencies; PeaceBuilders (Flannery et al., 2003), on a measure of interpersonal competencies; and Social Problem Solving (Gottfredson, Jones, and Gore, 2002), on a measure of academic attainment. We have not included these eight interventions on our list of evidence-based interventions.

Overall, we identified 60 evidence-based SEL interventions under ESSA evidence requirements: We identified at least one statistically significant positive result and no statistically significant negative results (i.e., "countervailing evidence") on an outcome of interest.

Outcomes Affected by Evidence-Based SEL Interventions

Examples of constructs, by domain, include the following:

- *intrapersonal competencies:* attention, concentration, emotional regulation, on-task behaviors, coping skills, self-esteem, self-efficacy, and perseverance
- *interpersonal competencies:* hostile attribution biases, attitudes toward violence, social information processing, aggression, prosocial behaviors, interpersonal communication, and social problem-solving skills

- *academic achievement:* standardized assessments on mathematics, reading, writing, and vocabulary
- *academic attainment:* attendance, completion of core courses, and graduation rates
- *disciplinary outcomes:* disciplinary code violations, disciplinary referrals, and suspensions
- *civic attitudes and behaviors:* tolerance of and empathy for others, interest in other countries and current events, and beliefs in a moral order
- *school climate and safety:* perceptions of classroom supportiveness and school safety, students' feelings of inclusion, quality of student-teacher relationships, and witnessing and perpetrating bullying.

Across all interventions, the outcome domains most commonly affected were interpersonal and intrapersonal competencies (Figure 5.1): Forty-two interventions (70 percent) had a statistically significant positive result for at least one measure of interpersonal competencies, while 31 (52 percent) had a statistically significant positive result for at least one measure of intrapersonal competencies. The most commonly affected domains thereafter were school climate and safety (27 percent of interventions), academic achievement (15 percent), disciplinary outcomes (12 percent), academic attainment (10 percent), and civic attitudes and behaviors (7 percent). Interventions had a statistically significant result for two outcome domains on average, although the number of outcome domains positively affected by an intervention ranged from one to all seven.

Evidence Across School Levels

We found evidence meeting Tiers I through III for 40 interventions (67 percent) evaluated at the elementary school level, 21 interventions (35 percent) at the middle school level, and eight interventions (13 percent) at the high school level. Eight of these interventions (13 percent) were evaluated across multiple school levels (see Figure 5.2). The larger number of evidence-based interventions for elementary schools is con-

Figure 5.1
Outcome Domains with Statistically Significant Positive Results Across Evidence Tiers

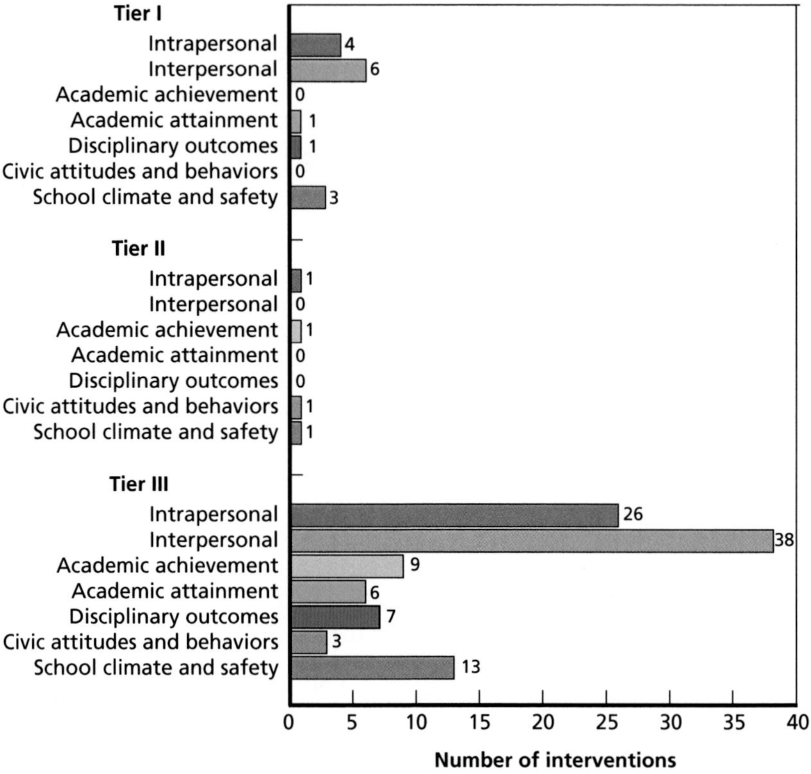

RAND *RR2133-5.1*

sistent with other research that has found fewer effects for skills-based, explicit SEL interventions among adolescents than among younger students (Heckman and Kautz, 2013; Yeager, 2017).

Among the 40 interventions evaluated at the elementary school level, we identified positive results most frequently for interpersonal competencies (80 percent of elementary school interventions), followed by intrapersonal competencies (53 percent), school climate and safety (28 percent), academic achievement (15 percent), disciplinary outcomes (10 percent), academic attainment (5 percent), and civic attitudes and behaviors (5 percent).

Figure 5.2
Tiers of Evidence for Interventions Across School Levels

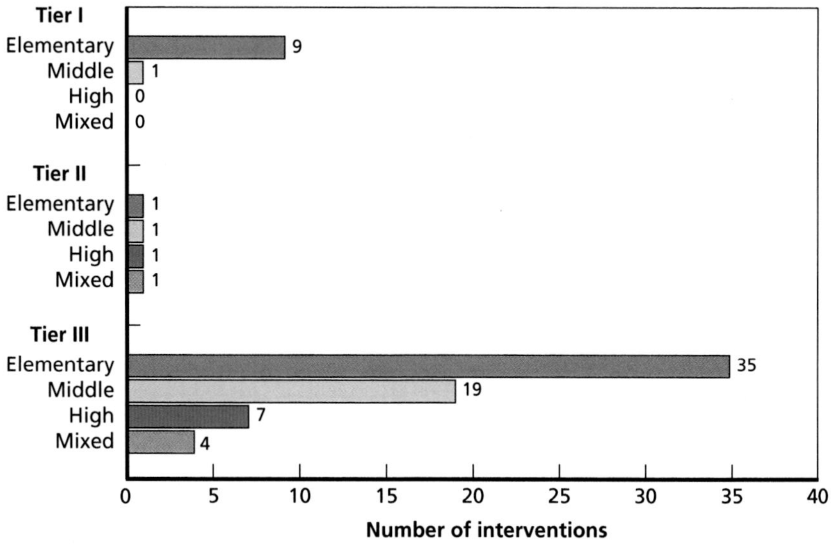

RAND *RR2133-5.2*

Among the 21 interventions evaluated at the middle school level, we identified positive results most frequently for interpersonal and intrapersonal competencies (57 percent of middle school interventions), followed by school climate and safety (33 percent), disciplinary outcomes (29 percent), academic attainment (19 percent), civic attitudes and behaviors (14 percent), and academic achievement (10 percent).

Among the 8 interventions evaluated at the high school level, we identified positive results most frequently for intrapersonal competencies (50 percent of high school interventions), followed by interpersonal competencies (38 percent), civic attitudes and behaviors (25 percent), academic achievement and attainment (13 percent), and school climate and safety (13 percent).

Samples and Settings of the Evaluations

When setting was reported, interventions were most commonly evaluated in urban communities (68 percent of interventions), followed by suburban (28 percent) and rural (20 percent) communities (see Figure 5.3). In addition, 40 interventions (67 percent) had at least one evaluation with a sample predominantly consisting of students classified as members of racial or ethnic minority groups, and 41 interventions (68 percent) had at least one evaluation with a sample predominantly consisting of economically disadvantaged students.

Key Intervention Components

Overall, most interventions (78 percent) involved teachers as implementers, followed by support staff (43 percent), counselors (35 percent), and administrators (20 percent). All interventions included explicit instruction (i.e., teaching, modeling, practicing, and/or applying social and emotional competencies; Durlak et al. 2011). In the vast majority of interventions (93 percent), this instruction involved class-

Figure 5.3
Tiers of Evidence for Interventions Across Settings

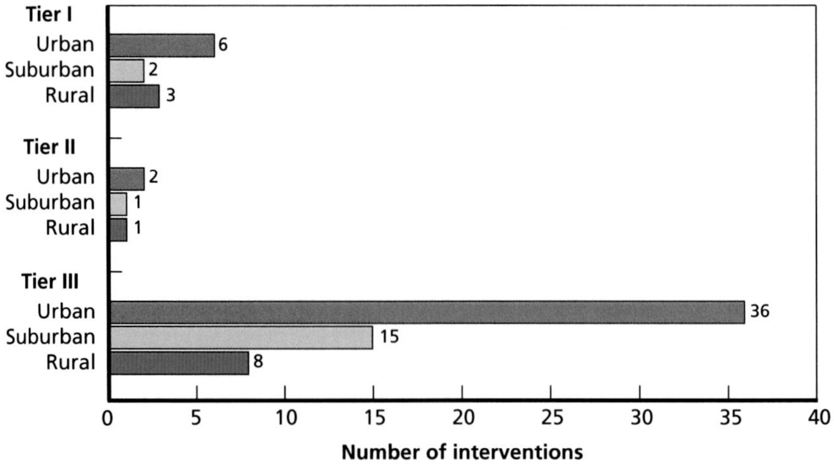

RAND *RR2133-5.3*

room curriculum to help students develop social and emotional competencies. In addition, a significant proportion of interventions (47 percent) involved components to change the classroom environment to be more conducive to the development of social and emotional competencies. Components that involved family or community members (33 percent) or involved application of social and emotional competencies outside the classroom setting (28 percent) were less common. Six interventions (10 percent) reported an out-of-school-time component, such as summer camps (Catalano et al., 2003) or after-school activities (Bleeker et al., 2012; Chang and Muñoz, 2006; White, 2012). Most of the intervention evaluations involved some component related to the professional development of (77 percent) or implementation support for (87 percent) those delivering the intervention as part of the evaluation. A majority of the interventions (67 percent) have a dedicated website with more-detailed information for educators about the intervention.

Summary

This evidence review entailed a comprehensive search of recent research literature and a rigorous process for identifying studies, extracting study information, and classifying the evidence according to ESSA's tiers. We identified numerous SEL interventions across grade levels and school levels that have positive results on intrapersonal and interpersonal outcomes and meet ESSA's I–III evidence tiers. Several interventions demonstrated effects on additional outcomes, such as academic attainment and achievement, disciplinary outcomes, and school climate and safety. Options exist for educators looking for SEL interventions that have been validated for students from racial or ethnic minority groups and low–socioeconomic status (SES) families, as well as for schools in urban, suburban, and rural communities. Many interventions with positive results include professional development for teachers and other school staff delivering the intervention. Tables 5.1 through 5.4 summarize our findings. We encourage educators, schools, districts, LEAs, and SEAs seeking specific SEL interventions to use the directions and evidence table in Appendix B, as well the detailed intervention summaries in our companion volume, to identify the evidence-based interventions under ESSA that meet their needs.

In the next chapter, we discuss how educators who want to document that an intervention they want to implement, but that has not yet been empirically evaluated, meets Tier IV evidence requirements.

Table 5.1
Evidence-Based SEL Interventions Validated at the Elementary School Level

Intervention	Grades	Key Components	Positive Results (Tier)
Playworks	4–5	• Classroom curriculum • Applications outside the classroom • Out-of-school time • Website	**Intrapersonal:** class readiness (I), on-task behavior (I), transitioning from recess to learning (I) **Climate/Safety:** bullying (I), inclusiveness (I), student ownership of recess activities (I), student safety (I), student use of positive language (I)
Tools for Getting Along	4–5	• Classroom curriculum • Professional development • Implementation support • Website	**Intrapersonal:** anger control (III), trait anger (III) **Interpersonal:** orientation to problem solving (I), rational problem solving (I), social problem solving (I)
We Have Skills!	K–3	• Classroom curriculum • Changing the learning environment • Family/community involvement • Professional development • Implementation support • Website	**Interpersonal:** social skills (I)
Class-Wide Function-Related Intervention Teams	K–5	• Classroom curriculum • Changing the learning environment • Professional development • Implementation support	**Intrapersonal:** on-task behavior (I)
Michigan Model for Health	4–5	• Classroom curriculum • Professional development • Implementation support • Website	**Interpersonal:** aggressive behavior (I), interpersonal communication (I), social and emotional skills (I)

Table 5.1—Continued

Intervention	Grades	Key Components	Positive Results (Tier)
Steps to Respect	3–6[a]	• Classroom curriculum • Applications outside the classroom • Family/community involvement • Professional development • Implementation support • Website	**Interpersonal:** agreeable social interactions (I), argumentative social interactions (I), assertiveness (I), nonbullying aggression (I), social competency (III) **Climate/Safety:** acceptance of bullying (I), bullying (I/III), bullying encouragement (I), bystander responsibility (I/III), exclusionary gossip (I), staff responsiveness to bullying (I/III), student responsiveness to bullying (III), student climate (III), target of bullying (I)
Social Skills Improvement System—Classwide Intervention Program	2	• Classroom curriculum • Professional development • Implementation support • Website	**Intrapersonal:** academic motivation (I), academic engagement (I), classroom engagement (I), responsibility (I), self-control (I) **Interpersonal:** communication (I), cooperation (I), empathy (I), social skills (I) **Climate/Safety:** disruptive classroom environment (I)
Too Good for Violence	3	• Classroom curriculum • Changing the learning environment • Implementation support • Website	**Intrapersonal:** emotional competency (III) **Interpersonal:** communication skills (III), inappropriate social behavior (III), prosocial behavior (III), resistance skills (III), social adaptability (III), social skills (III)
Raising Healthy Children	1–2	• Changing the learning environment • Out-of-school time • Family/community involvement • Professional development • Implementation support • Website	**Intrapersonal:** commitment to school (III) **Interpersonal:** antisocial behavior (III), social competency (III)

Table 5.1—Continued

Intervention	Grades	Key Components	Positive Results (Tier)
PATHS	1–6[a]	• Classroom curriculum • Changing the learning environment • Applications outside the classroom • Family/community involvement • Professional development • Implementation support • Website	**Intrapersonal:** cognitive concentration (III), cognitive regulation (III) **Interpersonal:** aggressive interpersonal negotiation strategies (III), aggressive social problem solving (III), authority acceptance (III), conduct problems (III), hostile attribution bias (III), problem behaviors (III), social competence (III) **Achievement:** mathematics (III), reading (III), writing (III)
PRAISE	3–4	• Classroom curriculum • Implementation support	**Interpersonal:** social problem solving (III)
Ready to Learn	K	• Classroom curriculum • Changing the learning environment • Professional development • Implementation support	**Intrapersonal:** listening comprehension (III) **Interpersonal:** behavior (III)
Social Aggression Prevention Program	4–6[a]	• Classroom curriculum • Professional development • Implementation support	**Interpersonal:** social problem-solving skills (III)
Tools of the Mind	K	• Changing the learning environment • Professional development • Implementation support • Website	**Intrapersonal:** cognitive flexibility (III), inhibitory control (III), working memory (III) **Achievement:** mathematics (III), reading (III), vocabulary (III)

Table 5.1—Continued

Intervention	Grades	Key Components	Positive Results (Tier)
INSIGHTS	K–2	• Classroom curriculum • Changing the learning environment • Family/community involvement • Professional development • Implementation support • Website	**Intrapersonal:** attention (III) **Interpersonal:** behavior problems at home (III), behavior problems at school (III) **Achievement:** mathematics (III), reading (III) **Climate/Safety:** classroom emotional support (III)
Bullying Literature Project	3–4	• Classroom curriculum • Applications outside the classroom • Family/community involvement • Professional development • Implementation support	**Interpersonal:** prosocial behavior (III)
4Rs	3–4	• Classroom curriculum • Changing the learning environment • Professional development • Implementation support • Website	**Interpersonal:** aggressive behavior (III), hostile attribution bias (III), socially competent behavior (III)
Youth Matters	4–5	• Classroom curriculum • Changing the learning environment • Applications outside the classroom • Professional development • Implementation support	**Climate/Safety:** victimization (III)

Table 5.1—Continued

Intervention	Grades	Key Components	Positive Results (Tier)
Friend to Friend	3–5	• Classroom curriculum • Applications outside the classroom • Implementation support	**Interpersonal:** prosocial behavior (III) **Climate/Safety:** student-teacher relationships (III)
Good Behavior Game	1–3	• Changing the learning environment • Family/community involvement • Professional development • Implementation support • Website	**Achievement:** mathematics (III), reading (III)
Resolving Conflict Creatively Program	1–6[a]	• Classroom curriculum • Changing the learning environment • Applications outside the classroom • Family/community involvement • Professional development • Implementation support • Website	**Interpersonal:** aggressive behavior (III), aggressive interpersonal negotiation strategies (III), competent interpersonal negotiation strategies (III), conduct problems (III), hostile attribution bias (III), prosocial behavior (III)
Responsive Classroom	2–5	• Changing the learning environment • Applications outside the classroom • Professional development • Implementation support • Website	**Interpersonal:** assertion (III), prosocial behavior (III) **Achievement:** mathematics (III), reading (III)

Table 5.1—Continued

Intervention	Grades	Key Components	Positive Results (Tier)
Bully-Proofing Your School	3–5	• Classroom curriculum • Changing the learning environment • Applications outside the classroom • Family/community involvement • Professional development • Implementation support • Website	**Interpersonal:** physical aggression perpetration (III), relational aggression perpetration (III) **Climate/Safety:** physical aggression victimization (III), relational aggression victimization (III), witnessing aggression (III), discouragement of bullying at school (III), perceived school safety (III)
Open Circle	4	• Classroom curriculum • Changing the learning environment • Family/community involvement • Implementation support • Website	**Interpersonal:** problem behavior (III), social skills (III)
Caring School Communities	3–5	• Classroom curriculum • Changing the learning environment • Applications outside the classroom • Out-of-school time • Family/community involvement • Professional development • Implementation support • Website	**Climate/Safety:** classroom supportiveness (III), student autonomy (III), trust in students (III)

Table 5.1—Continued

Intervention	Grades	Key Components	Positive Results (Tier)
Skills for Growing	3–5	• Classroom curriculum • Applications outside the classroom • Out-of-school time • Family/community involvement • Professional development • Implementation support • Website	**Interpersonal:** relationship skills (III) **Disciplinary:** minimally disruptive behavior (III) **Climate/Safety:** safe and respectful climate (III)
I Can Problem Solve	K–1	• Classroom curriculum • Changing the learning environment • Professional development • Implementation support • Website	**Interpersonal:** prosocial behavior (III), overt aggression (III), relational aggression (III)
Talking with TJ	3	• Classroom curriculum • Changing the learning environment • Family/community involvement • Professional development • Implementation support • Website	**Intrapersonal:** self-concept (III)
Urban Improv	4	• Classroom curriculum • Website	**Intrapersonal:** hyperactivity (III), self-control (III) **Interpersonal:** cooperative behavior (III), externalizing behavior (III)

Table 5.1—Continued

Intervention	Grades	Key Components	Positive Results (Tier)
RULER	5–6[a]	• Classroom curriculum • Professional development • Implementation support • Website	**Intrapersonal:** school problems (III) **Interpersonal:** social adaptability (III)
Strong Kids	3–4	• Classroom curriculum • Changing the learning environment • Professional development • Implementation support • Website	**Intrapersonal:** emotional competencies/assets (III) **Interpersonal:** social coping skills (III), social functioning (III)
Making Choices	3	• Classroom curriculum • Changing the learning environment • Professional development • Implementation support • Website	**Intrapersonal:** cognitive concentration (III) **Interpersonal:** encoding social information (III), hostile attribution (III), overt aggression (III), peer acceptance (III), prosocial goal formulation (III), responsible decisionmaking (III), social aggression (III), social competence (III), social contact (III)
Competent Kids, Caring Communities	4–5	• Classroom curriculum • Changing the learning environment • Applications outside the classroom • Professional development • Implementation support • Website	**Intrapersonal:** attention/concentration (III), compliance (III), self-efficacy (III) **Interpersonal:** aggression (III), prosocial problem-solving skills (III), social/emotional competence (III)

[a] Elementary school includes 6th grade in this study.

Table 5.2
Evidence-Based SEL Interventions Validated at the Middle School Level

Intervention	Grades	Key Components	Positive Results (Tier)
Take the Lead	7	• Classroom curriculum • Family/community involvement • Professional development	**Climate/Safety:** bullying (III), victimization (III)
School-to-Jobs	8	• Classroom curriculum • Family/community involvement • Professional development • Implementation support	**Intrapersonal:** academic mindset (III), initiative taking (III) **Achievement:** standardized tests passed (III) **Attainment:** absences (III)
Go Grrrls	7	• Classroom curriculum • Professional development • Implementation support • Website	**Intrapersonal:** self-efficacy (III), self-esteem (III) **Interpersonal:** assertiveness (III), friendship esteem (III)
Mental Contrasting with Implementation Intentions	5[a]	• Classroom curriculum	**Intrapersonal:** preparedness for school (III) **Attainment:** attendance (III)
School/Community Intervention	5–8[a]	• Classroom curriculum • Applications outside the classroom • Family/community involvement • Professional development • Implementation support • Website	**Interpersonal:** provoking behavior (III), violent behavior (III) **Disciplinary:** school delinquency (III)

Table 5.2—Continued

Intervention	Grades	Key Components	Positive Results (Tier)
Social Development Curriculum	5–8[a]	• Classroom curriculum • Professional development • Implementation support • Website	**Interpersonal:** violent behavior (III)
Responding in Peaceful and Positive Ways	6–7	• Classroom curriculum • Professional development • Implementation support	**Interpersonal:** aggressive behavior (III), approval of nonviolent behavior (III), delinquent behavior (III), disapproval of violent behavior (III), nonviolent problem solving (III), physical aggression (III) **Disciplinary:** disciplinary code violations for violence (III) **Climate/Safety:** peer provocations (III), peer support for prosocial behavior (III), victimization and harassment (III)
Olweus Bullying Prevention Program	6–8	• Classroom curriculum • Changing the learning environment • Applications outside the classroom • Family/community involvement • Professional development • Implementation support • Website	**Climate/Safety:** perception that others will intervene (III)
Going for the Goal	7	• Classroom curriculum • Professional development • Implementation support	**Intrapersonal:** self-control (III) **Interpersonal:** social problem-solving skills (III)
RAP Club	7–8	• Classroom curriculum • Professional development • Implementation support	**Intrapersonal:** emotional self-regulation (III) **Interpersonal:** authority acceptance (III), social competence (III)

Table 5.2—Continued

Intervention	Grades	Key Components	Positive Results (Tier)
Taekwondo	7–8	• Classroom curriculum	**Interpersonal:** behavior control (III)
Project WIN	5[a]	• Classroom curriculum • Changing the learning environment • Implementation support	**Interpersonal:** conflict resolution skills (III)
Promoting Positive Peer Relationships	7–8	• Classroom curriculum • Professional development • Implementation support • Website	**Climate/Safety:** attitudes toward bullying (III), peer supports against bullying (III)

[a] Middle school includes 5th grade in this study.

Table 5.3
Evidence-Based SEL Interventions Validated at the High School Level

Intervention	Grades	Key Components	Positive Results (Tier)
Building Assets—Reducing Risks	9	• Classroom curriculum • Changing the learning environment • Applications outside the classroom • Family/community involvement • Professional development • Implementation support • Website	**Achievement:** mathematics (III), reading (III) **Attainment:** no failed course credits (III), number of core course credits (III)
Conflict Resolution and Peer Mediation	9	• Classroom curriculum • Implementation support	**Interpersonal:** attitudes toward conflict resolution (III), negotiation skills (III)
Real Lives	9–10	• Classroom curriculum	**Civic:** ethnocultural empathy (III), interest in current events (III), interest in other countries (III)
KnowConflict	9	• Classroom curriculum	**Interpersonal:** attitudes toward violence (III)
Violence Prevention Project	9–10	• Classroom curriculum • Professional development • Implementation support • Website	**Intrapersonal:** academic self-concept (III) **Interpersonal:** conflict resolution strategies (III)
Quiet Time	9	• Classroom curriculum • Website	**Intrapersonal:** resilience (III)

Table 5.4
Evidence-Based SEL Interventions Validated Across School Levels

Intervention	Grades	Key Components	Positive Results (Tier)
Second Step	K–8	• Classroom curriculum • Professional development • Implementation support • Website	**Intrapersonal:** hyperactivity (I), learning skills (I) **Interpersonal:** antisocial behavior (III), conduct problems (I), physical aggression (I), social competence (III) **Attainment:** absences (III)
Connect with Kids	7–12	• Classroom curriculum • Family/community involvement • Professional development • Implementation support • Website	**Intrapersonal:** intrapersonal character traits (II) **Civic:** civic character traits (II) **Climate/Safety:** perceived character of classmates (II)
Positive Action	1–8	• Classroom curriculum • Changing the learning environment • Applications outside the classroom • Family/community involvement • Professional development • Implementation support • Website	**Intrapersonal:** academic behaviors (III), academic motivation (III), disaffection with learning (III), self-concept (III), self-control (III), self-esteem (III) **Interpersonal:** aggressive problem solving (III), beliefs supportive of aggression (III), conduct problems (III), deviant peer affiliation (III), prosocial interactions (III), prosocial peer affiliation (III), social-emotional skills (III) **Achievement:** mathematics (II), reading (II) **Attainment:** absences (I), retention (III) **Disciplinary:** suspensions (I), referrals (III) **Civic:** honesty (III), morality (III) **Climate/Safety:** bullying behaviors (III), student safety and well-being (III), verbal and physical harassment at school (III)

Table 5.4—Continued

Intervention	Grades	Key Components	Positive Results (Tier)
Mindfulness Training	1–3 5–8	• Classroom curriculum • Implementation support	**Intrapersonal:** attention (III), selective attention (III), self-hostility (III), test anxiety (III), working memory capacity (III) **Interpersonal:** negative social coping strategies (III), rumination to cope with social situations (III), social skills (III)
Student Success Skills	5 7	• Classroom curriculum • Changing the learning environment • Professional development • Implementation support • Website	**Intrapersonal:** cognitive regulation (III), emotion control (III), self-awareness (III) **Interpersonal:** prosocial behavior (III) **Achievement:** mathematics (III), reading (III) **Climate/Safety:** bullying (III), class climate (III), classmate support (III)
Yoga	4–6 9 11–12	• Classroom curriculum • Changing the learning environment • Out-of-school time • Professional development • Implementation support • Website	**Intrapersonal:** anger control (III), coping skills (III), emotional regulation (III), resilience (III), school engagement (III), self-regulation (III), stress management (III) **Attainment:** absences (III) **Disciplinary:** detention (III)
Success for Kids	1–8	• Classroom curriculum • Out-of-school time • Professional development • Implementation support • Website	**Intrapersonal:** hyperactivity (III), self-esteem (III), study skills (III) **Interpersonal:** behavioral problems (III), communication (III), externalizing problems (III), social adaptability (III), social skills (III) **Disciplinary:** school problems (III) **Civic:** leadership competencies (III)

Table 5.4—Continued

Intervention	Grades	Key Components	Positive Results (Tier)
Peacemakers	4–8	• Classroom curriculum • Changing the learning environment • Applications outside the classroom • Professional development • Implementation support	**Interpersonal:** aggressive behavior (III) **Disciplinary:** disciplinary incidents for aggressive behavior (III), referral to conflict mediation (III), suspensions (III)

CHAPTER SIX

Guidance for Tier IV Interventions

In Chapter Five, we presented the SEL interventions that we identified as meeting ESSA evidence Tiers I, II, and III. However, the legislation also allows SEAs, LEAs, districts, schools, and other education stakeholders (hereafter we refer to either "SEAs" or "LEAs" for conciseness) to implement Tier IV interventions. In this chapter, we provide guidance on meeting Tier IV requirements for SEL interventions.

Tier IV Requirements

As presented in Chapter Three, ESSA defines an intervention that meets Tier IV requirements as

> an activity, strategy, or intervention that . . .
>
> (i)(I) demonstrates a rationale based on high-quality research findings or positive evaluation that such activity, strategy, or intervention is likely to improve student outcomes or other relevant outcomes; and
>
> (II) includes ongoing efforts to examine the effects of such activity, strategy, or intervention. (Public Law 114-95, Title VIII, Sec. 8002(21)(A)(ii), 2015)

The nonregulatory guidance from the U.S. Department of Education further explains Tier IV. First, the guidance suggests that, to *demonstrate a rationale*, an intervention should include a "well-specified logic model that is informed by research or an evaluation that suggests how the intervention is likely to improve *relevant outcomes*" (U.S. Department of Education, 2016, p. 9; emphasis in the original). In this context, a *logic model* is a visual representation of an intervention's theory of change, or the hypothesized processes through which an intervention's resources and activities affect the targeted outcomes. Second, the guidance suggests that, to meet Tier IV, there should be an "effort to study the effects of the intervention, ideally producing promising evidence or higher" (U.S. Department of Education, 2016, p. 9). An effort to study the effects of an intervention might include an ongoing evaluation of the intervention conducted by either the LEA implementing the program or another stakeholder.

While selecting an intervention that meets evidence Tiers I–III is usually preferable, it is possible that the LEA wants to implement an intervention that does not have evidence in Tiers I–III (such as those in Chapter Five). For example, an LEA or school may be unable to find an intervention designed for the population it serves and the outcomes it wishes to target, or the intervention that best suits its needs may require unavailable resources or capacities. Alternatively, an LEA may have already implemented or created an intervention for which no Tier I–III evidence exists. Tier IV was designed to give LEAs the flexibility to implement interventions that meet their needs but have not yet been studied widely, as well as to encourage local experimentation to examine the effects of emerging interventions and add to the overall evidence base. In this way, selecting a Tier IV intervention has been referred to an "evidence-building opportunity" (Lee et al., 2016, p. 14).

Selecting an Intervention

When selecting an intervention, an LEA or school should first conduct a needs assessment to determine its target population (e.g., grade levels, types of students) and target outcomes (e.g., intrapersonal competencies, school climate).[1] LEAs and schools should make efforts to gather

---

[1] Although this chapter focuses on Tier IV, some of the content applies to interventions at any evidence tier.

information from multiple stakeholders (e.g., teachers, students, parents, community members) to understand their local needs and the reasons for the needs more comprehensively. LEAs and schools should also consider their local capacity (including the available resources or practitioners' preferences and skills) when selecting an intervention to implement. In doing so, an LEA or school may be more likely to select an intervention that is aligned with the local context and can be sustained over time. Guidance to help LEAs or schools select interventions best suited to their needs is increasingly available online (Lee et al., 2016).

After taking these steps, an LEA or school that is unable to find an intervention with Tier I–III evidence that addresses the identified needs might choose to implement an intervention that meets Tier IV requirements. The following subsections discuss how to demonstrate a rationale and include an ongoing effort to examine the effects of the selected intervention.

Logic Model Demonstrating a Rationale

To meet the first condition of Tier IV, an intervention must demonstrate a research-based rationale describing why it is likely to improve student outcomes or other relevant outcomes. The recommended format for demonstrating and communicating this rationale is through a logic model. The Education Department General Administration Regulations (EDGAR) defines a *logic model* as

> a well-specified conceptual framework that identifies key components of the proposed process, product, strategy, or practice (i.e., the active "ingredients" that are hypothesized to be critical to achieving the relevant outcomes) and describes the relationships among the key components and outcomes, theoretically and operationally. (Code of Federal Regulations, Title 34, Sec. 77.1, 2015)

An effective logic model should draw on past research to detail the components of the intervention and provide empirical justification for the hypothesized ways these components affect the targeted outcomes.

That is, logic models are effective tools for visually communicating to stakeholders what an intervention entails and why it should work.

While there is no gold standard for how to design a logic model and what to present in it, most logic models contain similar information (see Figure 6.1) about *resources*, or the inputs required for implementation (e.g., materials, personnel, physical space, financial investments); *activities*, or the specific actions involved in implementation; *outputs*, or the observable products or direct results of the activities (e.g., number of lessons taught or number of tasks participants complete); and *outcomes*, or expected effects in the short, intermediate, and long terms on target skills, behaviors, or competencies.

Our example logic model for a generic schoolwide SEL intervention aims to make the logic model definitions in EDGAR and the nonregulatory guidance more concrete. However, this is just one possible illustration and certainly not the only option for designing a logic model. In this example, the first column in the figure details the key resources for the intervention, including the school staff responsible for implementing and supporting the intervention, the intervention materials, and existing school policies. These resources are used to enact the intervention activities listed in the second column. Some of the activities include classroom instruction on social and emotional competencies, schoolwide assemblies, and activities to engage parents in the intervention. These activities result in measurable outputs, such as completed classroom lessons on competencies and parents' receipt of information on the SEL intervention. The logic model hypothesizes that the activities and subsequent outputs will affect the target outcomes, listed in the last three columns. In the short term, this SEL intervention is expected to lead to increased intrapersonal and interpersonal competencies for students. Intermediate and long-term outcomes include improved classroom climate and increased academic achievement. At the bottom of the figure, we have included a discussion of contextual factors likely to affect the implementation of a schoolwide SEL intervention, such as baseline school climate and culture, as well as schoolwide instructional supports. The content of this box in the figure is an important reminder that, as an LEA plans for implementation, it must not only consider the newly selected intervention but also how

Figure 6.1
Example Logic Model for a Schoolwide SEL Intervention

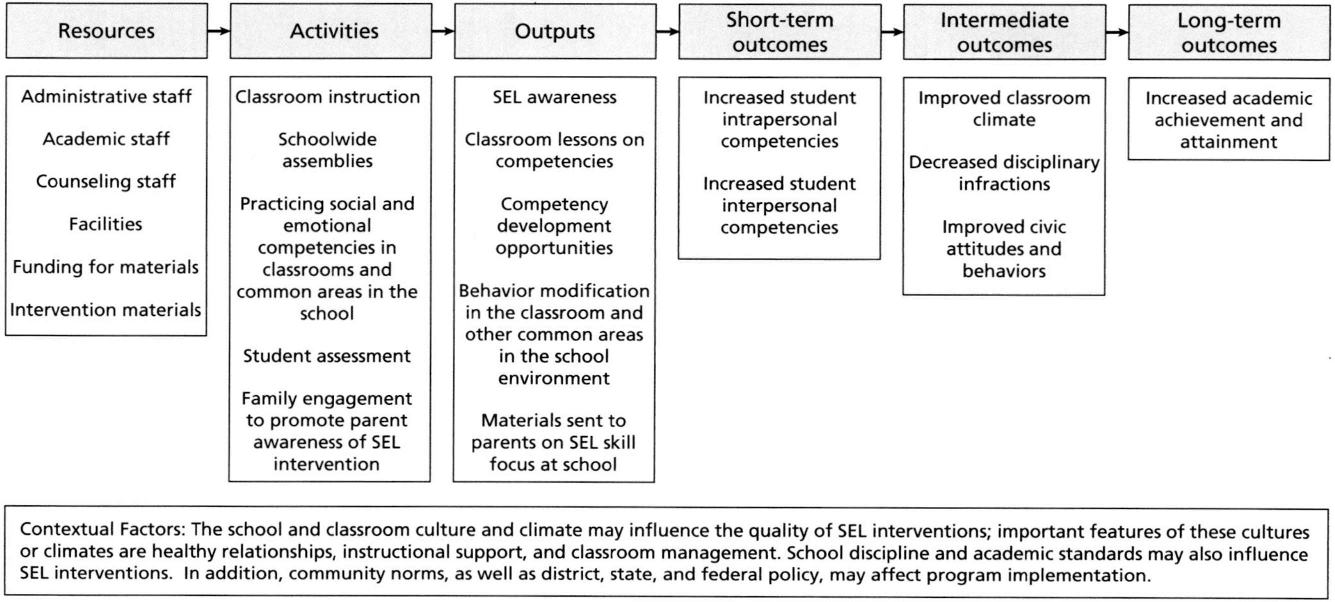

RAND *RR2133-6.1*

the intervention aligns with the existing characteristics and context of the school community.

Many intervention developers include logic models with program materials. An LEA trying to determine whether an intervention meets Tier IV requirements should consider searching intervention websites, program manuals, published research articles, and other available materials for a logic model. LEAs might also consider developing their own logic models for selected interventions, though doing so requires significant familiarity with the intervention components, target outcomes, and the theory and past research that connect the two. Freely available online materials provide a quick and user-friendly introduction to logic models and reference guides for using them as tools to help education stakeholders plan and monitor intervention evaluations; see box on p. 65 for examples.

Ongoing Effort to Evaluate the Intervention

To meet the second condition of Tier IV, there must be ongoing efforts to study the effects of a selected intervention. The nonregulatory guidance suggests that any ongoing research or evaluation efforts should be designed to produce at least Tier III ("promising") evidence for the intervention. As described in Chapter Three, Tier III evidence involves a well-implemented correlational study that compares students who received the intervention (a treatment group) with students who did not (a comparison group). To meet Tier III standards, a study design must methodologically or statistically adjust for nonrandom sorting of students into the treatment and comparison groups. These studies must thus account for factors—such as a student's gender, race or ethnicity, prior test scores, and parent education level—that might be related to the outcomes of interest *and* must partially explain students' membership in the treatment and comparison groups. While promising evidence is acceptable, ongoing research efforts that produce Tier I ("strong") or II ("moderate") evidence are preferred. Meeting these standards requires more-rigorous study designs, such as RCTs and quasi-experiments (corresponding to Tiers I and II, respectively). By mitigating the threat of selection bias, these studies provide more-reliable evidence of a program's effectiveness.

Resources on Logic Models and Program Evaluation

The following resources are freely available online; links are available in the bibliography:

1. Logic Models: A Tool for Designing and Monitoring Program Evaluations (Lawton et al., 2014)
   - Includes: a step-by-step guide on how to create a logic model
   - Developer: IES Regional Education Laboratory (REL) Program
2. Education Logic Model Application (REL Pacific, undated)
   - Includes: videos, guides, and application on logic models
   - Developer: IES REL Program
3. Logic Models for Program Design, Implementation, and Evaluation: Workshop Toolkit (Shakman and Rodriguez, 2015)
   - Includes: materials from a workshop on logic model design
   - Developer: IES REL Program
4. Logic Models to Support Program Design, Implementation and Evaluation (Shakman, 2014)
   - Includes: information on the value and components of a logic model
   - Developer: IES REL Program
5. A Practical Guide on Designing and Conducting Impact Studies in Education (Song and Herman, 2009)
   - Includes: a comprehensive report on experimental and quasi-experimental research studies
   - Developer: American Institutes for Research
6. RCT-YES (Mathematica Policy Research, 2016)
   - Includes: a freely available software package for program evaluation
   - Developer: Mathematica Policy Research
7. Program Development and Evaluation (University of Wisconsin–Extension, 2016)
   - Includes: written guides on logic models and program evaluation
   - Developer: University of Wisconsin-Extension
8. W.K. Kellogg Foundation Logic Model Development Guide (W.K. Kellogg Foundation, 2006)
   - Includes: a step-by-step guide on logic models and program evaluation
   - Developer: University of Kansas Work Group for Community Health and Development
9. Community Tool Box (Center for Community Health and Development, 2017)
   - Includes: materials explaining how to create and use a logic model in community programs
   - Developer: University of Kansas Work Group for Community Health and Development

To meet the ongoing evaluation condition for Tier IV, an LEA might select an intervention that is already being studied or evaluated by another organization, researcher, or stakeholder, even if the studied intervention is being implemented in a different LEA or other setting. To determine whether there are ongoing studies on a program of interest, an LEA can inquire with the intervention developer or use resources from IES (IES, undated a) and its REL Program (IES, undated b) to search for new research. Alternatively, an LEA may choose to design and execute its own evaluation of an intervention as part of an implementation plan. Doing so would take advantage of the Tier IV evidence-building opportunity by contributing new knowledge about the effects of an existing intervention. Designing a research study with the capacity to produce at least promising evidence involves extensive planning and input from many stakeholders. We suggest collaborating with school leaders, teachers, other school practitioners, parents, and community members. In addition, state data sources, other state-coordinated resources meant to support research and evaluation, and partnering with researchers at a local university or research organization can be used to bolster an LEA's research plans (Kane, 2017). Freely available online materials provide information about planning and running impact evaluations that meet WWC evidence standards; see box on p. 61 for examples.

Summary

Our review indicated that a variety of SEL interventions have evidence meeting the ESSA requirements for Tiers I through III. However, LEAs are not restricted to the interventions reviewed. Organizations may also consider interventions that meet Tier IV evidence. Tier IV evidence requires a demonstrated research-based rationale that describes why an intervention is likely to improve student outcomes or other relevant outcomes—in the form of a logic model—and there must be ongoing efforts to study the intervention's effects. ESSA's Tier IV provides additional flexibility and encourages local experimentation, which could ultimately enable states and LEAs to contribute to building the evidence base for SEL interventions and thereby expand the range of interventions that are available to future educators and policymakers across the United States. LEAs that are interested in adopting interventions that meet the Tier IV criteria should consider partnering with other LEAs and seeking guidance from the wide variety of resources that are available on the development of logic models and the design of evaluations.

In Chapter Seven, we summarize the key findings and recommendations from our report.

CHAPTER SEVEN

Key Findings and Recommendations

In this final chapter, we summarize several broad findings that emerged from our review. We then provide recommendations for practitioners and policymakers who are interested in leveraging ESSA funds to support students' SEL.

Key Findings

ESSA Offers Opportunities to Support SEL Through Several Different Funding Streams

The legislation does not include the phrase *social and emotional learning* but does provide multiple opportunities for states and LEAs to leverage federal funds for interventions that support SEL. Title I targets economically disadvantaged students. These funds can be used to support interventions and practices that improve academic and other relevant outcomes for these students and the schools that serve them, including social and emotional competencies. Title II focuses on recruitment, retention, and professional development of educators; SEAs and LEAs can use federal funds to prepare educators to deliver SEL interventions and assess social and emotional competencies. Title IV funds can be used to support several related goals, including a well-rounded education and the development of safe and healthy students, both inside and outside the school day.

Educators Have Many Options for SEL Interventions That Meet ESSA Evidence Requirements

Our review revealed a variety of SEL interventions that meet ESSA evidence requirements, facilitating the possibility of finding an evidence-based SEL intervention that meets local needs. As discussed in Chapter Five, most of the interventions we identified have demonstrated positive effects on intrapersonal and interpersonal outcomes; further, several ESSA-eligible interventions have also demonstrated positive effects on other important outcomes, such as academic achievement and school climate. Our review focused primarily on interventions that utilize explicit, freestanding instruction through which social and emotional competencies are explicitly taught. Educators have several options for interventions that help students develop these competencies through classroom curriculum, changing the learning environment, engaging family and community members, and providing opportunities to learn and practice competencies outside the classroom and in out-of-school-time contexts. More than 40 interventions have been validated on samples predominantly consisting of economically disadvantaged students targeted by Title I ESSA funds. Teachers are the primary providers for most identified interventions, and school staff received materials and/or professional development to deliver the intervention that could be supported by Title II ESSA funds in many evaluations. Educators can use our intervention lists in Appendix B to identify evidence-based SEL interventions, then use our detailed summaries of each ESSA-eligible intervention in our companion volume to select the interventions that best meet their local context and needs.

The Number of SEL Interventions That Meet ESSA Evidence Requirements Is Greatest for Elementary Schools and Urban Communities

Most of the interventions that we identified as meeting the strong, moderate, or promising evidence tiers (Tiers I–III) have been validated for use with elementary school students, with fewer options available for middle and high school students. This discrepancy is not surprising, especially given that explicit SEL interventions are more likely to target elementary than secondary students. In addition to school level, we also identified more ESSA-eligible SEL interventions for urban communities than for suburban and rural communities.

Although the reasons for these differences are not clear, one possible explanation for a greater number of SEL interventions for elementary school grade levels relates to the departmentalized nature of academic instruction and the tighter scheduling constraints at many middle and high schools. Because these schools' schedules might not accommodate free-standing lessons, educators may be more likely to address SEL through integration into academic instruction or school climate and discipline initiatives. They might also be more likely to deliver SEL-related interventions as part of programs focused on preventing high-risk behaviors (e.g., substance use) or targeted to at-risk students demonstrating social and emotional difficulties rather than universally to entire cohorts (e.g., classrooms or grade levels).

This difference also probably reflects differences in the extent to which explicit SEL instruction meets the developmental needs of students at different age levels. A review of research on SEL interventions with adolescents (Yeager, 2017) suggests that efforts to improve students' social and emotional competencies through direct instruction might not be the most effective with these students. Instead, interventions that emphasize students' mind-sets and the broader school climate appear to be the most promising, perhaps because they are more developmentally aligned with adolescents' needs, such as autonomy, respect from peers and adults, and a sense of competence.

These findings reinforce the need for educators to be judicious and cautious when considering the implementation of an intervention in grade or school levels significantly distant from those in which the intervention was validated. Both students' psychological development and the social and emotional demands of their environments differ significantly across school levels, making the developmental appropriateness of an intervention a key consideration for implementation. Educators should seriously consider whether the goals and competencies of an intervention match the targeted sample.

The prevalence of studies conducted in urban schools may be due in part to the fact that urban districts tend to be larger than other districts and therefore can accommodate larger studies; it is also possible that such districts are more amenable to SEL research because of a perceived need for evidence in this area.

Interpersonal Competencies Are the Most Common Outcomes Positively Impacted in Studies of Evidence-Based Interventions

Our review examined a range of student outcomes, but we found that most studies reported positive impacts on social and emotional competencies rather than on other outcomes, such as academic achievement. Of course, this focus is not unexpected, given the emphasis of SEL interventions on helping students improve these competencies. Of the two broad categories of social and emotional competencies we considered, interpersonal competencies (e.g., hostile attribution biases, prosocial behaviors, interpersonal communication, and social problem-solving skills) were more likely to be positively affected than intrapersonal competencies (e.g., attention, concentration, emotional regulation, and perseverance).

Recommendations for Educators and Policymakers

Conduct a Needs Assessment to Inform Decisions About SEL Interventions

Regardless of whether ESSA requires a needs assessment for drawing on a particular funding stream, schools and LEAs should consider carrying out assessments that can help determine what types of SEL interventions will meet local needs. This assessment might include direct measures of students' social and emotional competencies and broader measures of school climate or other relevant school-level conditions. A needs assessment can help ensure that limited resources are focused on the most important activities and that the selected interventions will be aligned with local needs and objectives. The nonregulatory guidance and the online resources we listed in Chapter Six provide further details on how to design and run a successful needs assessment.

Use the List of Interventions in This Review as a Starting Point

Our review provides a broad range of evidence-based interventions that educators can use as a resource. However, the results of this review should not be treated as a definitive list of approved options. Although the interventions identified in this review meet ESSA evidence requirements, it is possible that none of them will adequately address the needs of a specific set of students or schools. Moreover, even if an intervention does not currently meet ESSA requirements according to our review, such evidence might be available in the future, especially given the growing focus on research examining SEL interventions. Educators may also adapt an intervention to fit their own circumstances and goals, drawing on the evidence from the intervention to support a claim that their approach meets evidence Tiers I through III. To be as similar as possible to interventions as validated in Tier I through III evaluations, the replication should consider the key activities, strategies, and practices of the original intervention.

Take Advantage of Tier IV Flexibility if Needs Cannot Be Met by Interventions with Stronger Evidence

Although some funding streams require interventions to meet Tiers I through III, others permit the use of funds for Tier IV interventions. This provides opportunities for educators to draw on a wider range of interventions. It also allows educators to create new interventions or significantly adapt existing approaches to fit local contexts, provided creators can offer a research-based rationale and engage in ongoing evaluation of these efforts. LEA and school leaders could consider forming consortia to design and carry out evaluation activities and to learn from one another's efforts and should look to external resources, such as the RELs, for evaluation guidance.

Provide Professional Development and Other Supports to Build Educators' Capacity to Gather and Use Evidence of Program Effectiveness

Gathering and reading peer-reviewed literature to glean information about evidence is a time-consuming and resource-intensive process. In many cases, educators will not even have the opportunity to access relevant articles because the information sits behind paywalls established by academic journal publishers. Reports like this one, along with other related resources, such as the "Evidence for ESSA" webpage

(Center for Research and Reform in Education, 2017) and some of the REL resources, can reduce or, in some cases, eliminate the need for educators to review literature and assess the quality of evidence. SEAs and LEAs should consider ways to provide professional development, including coaching and professional learning communities, to promote educators' awareness of these resources and capacity to use the information the resources provide. Moreover, teachers or other educators expected to contribute to ongoing evaluation efforts will need guidance and opportunities to collaborate with colleagues to help design rigorous evaluations. One important but often overlooked resource is dedicated time for reading, collaborating, and engaging in other activities that will enable teachers and staff members to gather and use evidence to inform their practice.

Consider a Variety of SEL Programs and Strategies When Designing Approaches to Improving Students' Social and Emotional Competencies

As we discussed in Chapter One, explicit stand-alone programs are not the only way schools can promote social and emotional competencies. Other approaches include integration of SEL into academic instruction (e.g., by engaging students in historical debates that promote interpersonal competencies) and school climate or discipline programs that emphasize SEL skills. The ESSA funding streams that we summarized in Chapter Three can also be used to support these other strategies, so educators should consider how to create an integrated approach to addressing these social and emotional competencies, rather than focusing exclusively on a single program or curriculum. This approach should be aligned across grade levels to the extent possible, so that students experience a common, coherent approach to SEL throughout the school day and as they progress through school (O'Connor et al., 2017).

Address Local Conditions to Promote Effective SEL Implementation

Adopting an evidence-based intervention does not, of course, guarantee results that match those found in the reviewed research. One consideration for educators and policymakers who adopt new interventions is the need to ensure that the broader conditions are in place to support high-quality intervention implementation. These conditions include high-quality, customized professional development; a supportive schoolwide culture; and district and school policies that provide time and resources for SEL interventions. In addition, external partners who provide technical assistance might help address these conditions and support implementation, although the quality of that support can vary. Guidance for promoting high-quality SEL implementation appears in several reports (Jones et al., 2017; O'Connor et al., 2017; Kendziora and Yoder, 2016), and we note in our companion volume which interventions have dedicated websites containing information on technical assistance and implementation support.

Continue to Improve SEL Measurement

The studies reviewed in this report relied on a variety of assessments of students' social and emotional competencies. Most of these measures have some evidence of reliability and validity for their intended uses, including for research purposes, but were not necessarily designed to support day-to-day instructional decisionmaking and continuous improvement efforts. Educators continue to lack access to high-quality assessments that meet their specific needs, particularly those that impose low burdens and costs. In addition to continuing to invest in high-quality intervention studies, funders and policymakers should prioritize efforts to improve measurement, particularly those efforts that involve collaborations between assessment developers and potential users who can provide guidance that will help ensure that the resulting tools meet educators' needs.

Provide Feedback on Evidence Tier Requirements

Due to remaining ambiguity in ESSA evidence requirements and variability in how states may interpret these requirements, we made several methodological decisions that may differ from other reviews identifying evidence-based interventions under ESSA and that may differ in the future should greater clarity or changes to the evidence requirements arise. In addition to ambiguities, some issues result from potential inconsistencies between WWC evidence standards and recommendations in the nonregulatory guidance on interpreting ESSA evidence

Looking Ahead

The flexibility built into ESSA, particularly with regard to Tier IV, offers extensive opportunities for future research that is informed by the needs and goals of local practitioners and policymakers. The potential for growth in evidence-based SEL interventions is great but will require collaborative efforts from researchers, educators, and policymakers at all levels to promote high-quality research and evaluation activities accompanied by dissemination strategies that make the findings widely accessible to potential users.

requirements (which recommends following WWC evidence standards for Tiers I and II). Because these ambiguities remain, we encourage educators to provide feedback to SEAs and the U.S. Department of Education about particularly pressing ambiguities in the evidence standards. Moving forward, we particularly encourage the exploration of more-stringent criteria for the highest evidence tiers and the promotion of established approaches for considering the body of evidence in decisionmaking (Guyatt et al. 2008; Alonso-Coello et al., 2016a; Alonso-Coello et al., 2016b). In addition, because some ambiguities stem from missing details in evaluation reports, we encourage evaluators to preregister their evaluations and report their evaluations more comprehensively (Grant et al., 2013) to increase the utility of the findings to educators.

APPENDIX A

Additional Technical Details for Evidence Review

Developing the Conceptual Framework

We consulted with key members of the Wallace Foundation and reviewed seminal work on SEL to establish the conceptual framework for our review. After reviewing several frameworks that categorized outcomes in SEL, we designed our conceptual framework around the categories from the NRC framework. The NRC framework classifies competencies into three broad domains—cognitive, intrapersonal, and interpersonal—each of which includes several clusters of competencies. We used this framework to design our review process because it encompasses a wide range of social and emotional competencies, associates broad clusters of competencies with specific constructs, and reflects consensus among experts who have studied SEL from a variety of disciplinary perspectives. We ultimately included all five clusters from the intrapersonal and interpersonal domains to form the basis of our SEL review framework—excluding any clusters from the NRC cognitive domain.

Search Strategy

We used the following general SEL search strings for ERIC (all other search strings are available upon request):

ERIC; all doc types; 2002 to 22 September 2016; English
"public school*" OR "Charter school*" OR "magnet school*" OR "primary school*" OR "elementary school*" OR "secondary school*" OR "middle school*" OR "high school*" OR "Grade school" OR "grade school*" OR kindergarten*

AND

TI bully* OR AB bully* OR TI "career orientation" OR AB "career orientation" OR TI "Character development" OR AB "Character development" OR TI "character education" OR AB "character education" OR TI citizenship OR AB citizenship OR TI "civic engagement" OR AB "civic engagement" OR TI civility OR AB civility OR TI collaboration OR AB collaboration OR TI "commun* responsibility" OR AB "commun* responsibility" OR TI competence OR AB competence OR TI conscientiousness OR AB conscientiousness OR TI "conflict resolution" OR AB "conflict resolution" OR TI "continuous learning" OR AB "continuous learning" OR TI cooperation OR AB cooperation OR TI courage OR AB courage OR TI "Decision making" OR AB "Decision making" OR TI "dropout prevention" OR AB "dropout prevention" OR TI "emotional development" OR AB "emotional development" OR TI "emotional intelligence" OR AB "emotional intelligence" OR TI "emotional learning" OR AB "emotional learning" OR TI empath* OR AB empath* OR TI "ethical development" OR AB "Ethical development" OR TI grit OR AB grit OR TI initiative OR AB initiative OR TI integrity OR AB integrity TI "intellectual openness" OR AB "intellectual openness" OR TI "interpersonal skills" OR AB "interpersonal skills" OR TI Leadership OR AB leadership OR TI motivation OR AB motivation OR TI "non-cognitive skills" OR AB "non-cognitive skills" OR TI Perseverance OR AB perseverance OR TI "positive youth development" OR AB "positive youth development" OT TI pro-social OR AB pro-social OR TI prosocial OR AB prosocial OR TI Resilience OR AB resilience OR TI responsibility OR TI Responsibility OR TI SEL OR AB SEL OR TI "self-evaluation" OR AB "Self-evaluation" OR TI "self-awareness" OR AB "self-awareness" OR TI "Self-direction" OR

AB "self-direction" OR TI "Self-reflection" OR AB "Self-reflection" OR TI "Self-regulation" OR AB "Self-regulation" OR TI "social and emotional learning" OR AB "Social and emotional learning" OR TI "Social-emotional learning" OR AB "Social-emotional learning" OR TI "Social awareness" OR AB "Social awareness" OR TI "Social development" OR AB "social development" OR TI "social emotional education" OR AB "Social emotional education" OR TI "social responsibility" OR AB "social responsibility" OR TI "social skills" OR AB "social skills" OR TI teamwork OR AB teamwork OR TI tolerance OR AB tolerance OR TI "whole child" OR AB "whole child" OR TI "work ethic" OR AB "work ethic" OR TI restorative OR AB restorative OR TI Reparation OR AB reparation OR TI respect OR AB respect OR TI reintegration OR AB reintegration OR TI circle OR AB circle OR TI Offender OR AB offender OR TI Conferencing OR AB conferencing

AND

"rigorous research" OR impact OR effect OR outcome OR "randomized control" OR RCT OR "quasi-experimental" OR RCT OR correlational OR quantitative OR "research synthesis" OR "meta analysis" OR review OR evaluat*
NOT
SU Foreign countries

Screening and Eligibility Assessment

We first screened the titles and abstracts of all retrieved citations. We uploaded all retrieved citations into the EPPI-Reviewer software for evidence synthesis (EPPI-Centre, 2017). Each citation was screened independently by two researchers (ten researchers in total were involved in title and abstract screening) using the following criteria:

- EXCLUDE on language: not published in English
- EXCLUDE on noneducation focus: does not address a topic related to education

- EXCLUDE on country: not in United States, its territories, and tribal communities (i.e., 50 states, Washington D.C., Bureau of Indian Education, Department of Defense Dependent Schools, Department of Defense Education Activity, American Samoa, Guam, Northern Mariana Islands, Puerto Rico, and U.S. Virgin Islands)
- EXCLUDE on date: manuscript published before 2002 or intervention implemented before 1994
- EXCLUDE on conference citation: conference abstract, presentation, panel, or paper
- EXCLUDE on publication type: OpEd; letter to the editor; newspaper, magazine, or newsletter article, book or book chapter, book review
- EXCLUDE on population age: either pre-K or postsecondary
- EXCLUDE on population status: not currently enrolled in public school
- EXCLUDE on setting: taking place outside K–12 public schools
- EXCLUDE on intervention status: unintended or unplanned actions and events that had an impact on SEL
- EXCLUDE on intervention purpose: interventions that were not primarily designed to address social and emotional competencies in the intrapersonal or interpersonal domains of the NRC framework
- EXCLUDE on intervention target: intervention targets parents, teachers, and/or school staff as participants (rather than students)
- EXCLUDE on special population: intervention focuses on K–12 students who are not an intact group, are a specially assembled "at-risk" group, or have a specific indication
- EXCLUDE on outcomes: study does not measure an outcome in at least one of the domains of interest (intrapersonal or interpersonal domains of the NRC framework, academic achievement in mathematics or English language arts and reading as measured by a standardized assessment, academic attainment, disciplinary outcomes, civic attitudes and behaviors, or school climate and safety)
- EXCLUDE on study method: not an empirical study meeting ESSA Tiers I–III

The research librarian obtained full texts for the citations that at least one reviewer deemed potentially eligible. Each full text we were able to retrieve was screened independently by two researchers (ten researchers in total were involved in full-text eligibility assessment) using the same criteria as for the title and abstract screening. We included each citation deemed eligible by both reviewers. Disagreements about eligibility were resolved by the review team. Overall, our search identified over 24,000 citations, of which 4,943 went through full-text eligibility assessment, yielding 150 manuscripts of eligible studies evaluating 68 SEL interventions. Of these 68 SEL interventions, 60 met ESSA Tiers I-III (see Figure A.1).

Data Extraction

For each included report, two researchers (ten researchers in total were involved in data extraction) independently extracted the following data when reported:

- study- and site-level characteristics
  - month and year: the month(s) and year(s) during which the study took place
  - geographic location: geographic location(s) of the study (e.g., city, state, region)
  - school district: school district(s) involved (e.g., number, names)
  - number of schools: number of schools involved in the study
  - number of classrooms: number of classrooms involved in the study
  - type of school: type of school(s) involved (e.g., charter, alternative)
  - grade levels served: grade levels served at the school(s) involved (e.g., pre-K to 6, K–8, 3–8)
  - school size (total enrollment): total enrollment of school(s) involved in the study
  - community status: urban, suburban, or rural status of school(s) involved in the study

Figure A.1
Flow of Literature Search

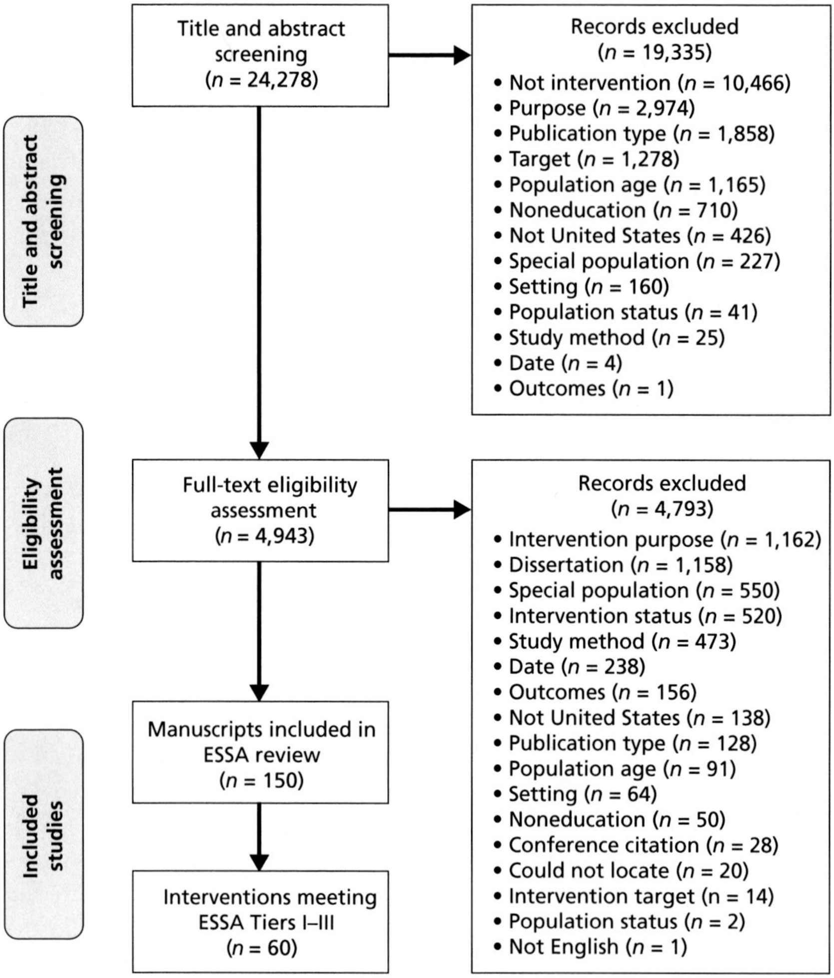

RAND *RR2133-A.1*

- district size: size of the district(s) involved in the study
- Title I: Title I status of the school(s) involved in the study
- low-income: low-income status of the school(s) involved in the study

  - students with disabilities: students with disabilities status of the school(s) involved in the study
  - English language learners: English language learner status of the school(s) involved in the study
  - race or ethnicity: race or ethnicity of students at the school(s) involved in the study
  - school climate ratings: climate at the school(s) involved in the study
  - school safety ratings: safety at the school(s) involved in the study
  - discipline rates: discipline rates at the school(s) involved in the study
  - attendance rates: attendance rates at the school(s) involved in the study
  - school-level English language arts and reading performance: reading performance rates at the school(s) involved in the study
  - school-level math performance: math rates at the school(s) involved in the study
- sample characteristics
  - recruitment procedures: how researchers recruited participants for the study
  - eligibility criteria: inclusion and exclusion criteria for students to be eligible for the study
  - sample size: full sample size and sample size for each intervention and comparison group
  - age: average age (standard deviation) for full sample and for each intervention and comparison group
  - sex or gender: percent female for full sample and for each intervention and comparator group
  - race or ethnicity: reported race or ethnicity data for full sample and for each intervention and comparator group
  - grade level: reported grade-level data for full sample and for each intervention and comparator group
  - income (including free- or reduced-price lunch): reported income data for full sample and for each intervention and comparator group

  - prior English language arts and reading achievement: reported data for full sample and for each intervention and comparator group
  - prior math achievement: reported data for full sample and for each intervention and comparator group
  - prior discipline issues: reported data for full sample and for each intervention and comparator group
  - prior absence and attendance: reported data for full sample and for each intervention and comparator group
  - prior SEL ratings: reported data for full sample and for each intervention and comparator group
  - English language learners: reported data for full sample and for each intervention and comparator group
  - students with disability: reported data for full sample and for each intervention and comparator group
  - gifted and talented students: reported data for full sample and for each intervention and comparator group
  - old for grade or retained in a prior grade: reported data for full sample and for each intervention and comparator group
- intervention and comparison group characteristics
  - name: name or a phrase that describes the intervention
  - theory of change: any rationale, theory, or goal of the elements essential to the intervention
  - materials: any physical or informational materials used in the intervention, including those provided to participants or used in intervention delivery or in training of intervention providers, as well as information on where the materials can be accessed (such as online appendix, URL)
  - procedures: each of the procedures, activities, and/or processes used in the intervention, including any enabling or support activities
  - providers: expertise, background, and any specific training given to intervention providers
  - format or modality: modes of delivery (such as face to face or by some other mechanism, such as internet or telephone) of the

intervention and whether it was provided individually or in a group
  - location and timing: type(s) of location(s) where the intervention occurred, including any necessary infrastructure or relevant features
  - amount: number of times the intervention was delivered and over what period, including the number of sessions; their schedule; and their duration, intensity, or dose
  - preplanned tailoring or adaptation: if the intervention was planned to be personalized, titrated, or adapted, describes the what, why, when, and how
  - post hoc modifications: if the intervention was modified during the course of the study, describes the changes (what, why, when, and how)
  - fidelity measurement: if intervention adherence or fidelity was assessed, describes how and by whom and whether any strategies were used to maintain or improve fidelity, describe them
  - fidelity data: if intervention adherence or fidelity was assessed, describes the extent to which the intervention was delivered as planned
  - cointerventions: other interventions delivered to the sample at the same time as the experimental SEL intervention(s)
- study methods
  - design: study design that most accurately summarizes how the participants have been assigned to intervention groups (individual-RCT, cluster-RCT, nonrandomized assignment by researchers, cohorts not assigned by researchers, noncohort concurrent comparison group)
  - participant assignment method: how participants were assigned to groups (e.g., nature of randomization)
  - allocation concealment: whether and how those who assigned participants to groups were unaware of the assignment sequence (mostly applicable only to RCTs)
  - baseline equivalence: any reported information about baseline equivalence

- blinding or masking: any information about blinding or masking participants, providers, and/or outcome assessors
- overall attrition: overall attrition from the study at each follow-up point
- differential attrition: differential attrition from the study at each follow-up point
- selective outcome reporting: any information about selective outcome reporting (e.g., evidence that the authors did not report an outcome of interest that they measured, or an analysis of interest that they conducted)
- power calculation: power calculations done for the study
- crossover or contamination: crossovers and/or contamination between intervention and comparison groups in the study
- analytic method: procedures used to estimate outcomes (covariates of interest include pretest of outcome measure or related measure in same domain if outcome measure is impossible to measure at baseline, grade level or age, sex or gender, student special status, community status, SES, race or ethnicity)
- intention-to-treat procedures: analysis procedures related to intention to treat versus per protocol or as treated

- outcome data
  - domain: relevant domain to assign the outcome measure (i.e., SEL, academic achievement, academic attainment, disciplinary outcome, civic attitudes and behaviors, school climate and safety)
  - measure: name of the measure used
  - validity: validity of the measure
  - reliability: reliability of the measure
  - time points: when the measure is made (e.g., postintervention, three months postintervention)
  - metric: metric of the measure (e.g., change from baseline, follow-up)
  - method of aggregation: method of aggregation of the measure (e.g., mean, percentage)

- mediation: whether there is a mediation analysis on at least one measure in this outcome domain
- result: statistical significance and direction of effect.

Classifying the Evidence

To assign study findings to ESSA tiers, we used the ESSA legislation itself, the nonregulatory guidance from the U.S. Department of Education, the EDGAR definition of *evidence-based* (U.S. Department of Education, 2017), and guidance from WWC on its procedures and standards (IES, 2014) for group designs:

- *Tier I:* We classified study findings as meeting Tier I if assignment of participants to the intervention or comparison group was determined through a random process and if the combination of overall and differential attrition was low using the liberal boundaries of attrition standards in the WWC handbook (IES, 2014). We also classified all study findings deemed to meet WWC standards without reservations in a WWC intervention report or single study review as meeting Tier I, so long as the sample size and site requirements for Tier I were met (see below).
- *Tier II:* We classified study findings as meeting Tier II if the baseline equivalence requirements of the WWC handbook (IES, 2014) were met for the analytic sample on either (1) a pretest in the same domain as the outcome or (2), if such a measure did not exist, on a measure of academic achievement and SES. We also classified all study findings deemed to meet WWC standards with reservations in a WWC intervention report or single study review as meeting Tier II, so long as the sample size and site requirements for Tier II were met (see below).
- *Tier III:* We classified study findings as meeting Tier III if they did not meet Tier I or II but had a predictor of intervention status or receipt in a statistical model (i.e., whether participants were assigned to or received the SEL intervention rather than a com-

parator intervention) and included some methodological or statistical control for selection bias.

- *Sample size and number of sites:* To be classified as either Tier I or Tier II, study findings also needed to be based on a large analytic sample (at least 350 students) and multiple sites (at least two districts, LEAs, localities, or states). An outcome could cumulatively meet the large sample (at least 350 students) and multisite (at least two districts, LEAs, localities, or states) sample requirements if multiple studies meeting the other requirements for the corresponding tier found a positive result for this outcome. We did not employ any sample size or site requirements for Tier III studies.
- *Outcome measures:* For all studies, we did not include outsscome measures that were clearly invalid, unreliable, overaligned with the SEL intervention, or not measured in the same manner for the intervention and comparison groups. To be consistent with the nonregulatory guidance from the U.S. Department of Education, we made these judgments using the WWC handbook (IES, 2014). The lead author had ultimate discretion for judging the eligibility of an outcome measure, based on the information reported in included studies.
- *Confounds:* Any studies meeting the WWC definition for a confounding factor (e.g., intervention and comparison groups each contain only a single unit) were ineligible for Tiers I and II but were assessed for eligibility of meeting Tier III requirements.
- *Results*: For each relevant outcome meeting Tiers I through III, we assessed whether study findings were statistically significant and favoring the SEL intervention ("positive"), not statistically significant ("ns"), or statistically significant and favoring the comparator intervention ("negative"). We used the statistical significance levels reported by the study authors unless they did not account for (1) clustering when there was a mismatch between the unit of assignment and unit of analysis and/or (2) multiple comparisons of impact on the same outcome measure. Following the WWC handbook (IES, 2014), we attempted to compute clustering-corrected statistical significance estimates if the authors did not account for clustering and the Benjamini-Hochberg correction if

the authors did not account for multiple comparisons on the same outcome measure. For studies meeting Tier I or II, results that were no longer statistically significant after accounting for clustering or adjusting for multiple comparisons were relegated to Tier III. When included studies reported sufficient data, we also calculated effect sizes according to the WWC handbook (IES, 2014) for outcomes meeting Tier I or II. To be consistent with WWC evidence standards, we did not calculate effect sizes for outcomes meeting Tier III unless they were downgraded due to the sample size or multisite requirement from the nonregulatory guidance. In addition to assigning each study finding to an evidence tier, we also assigned each intervention to an evidence tier based on the highest rating achieved by any outcome across all studies.

ESSA Evidence Requirements That Would Benefit from Further Clarity

Further clarification and confirmation would be particularly helpful for the following issues:

- whether more-stringent criteria for study designs than the WWC criteria are needed
- whether more-stringent criteria for outcome measures than the WWC criteria are needed
- whether corrections for multiple comparisons should be made to reduce the threat of type I errors
- what tier to assign (if any) when a study reports insufficient information to make a conclusive tier determination
- how similar study samples and settings need to be to those of the intended students and schools
- what features make a study "of the equivalent quality for making causal inferences" to a study meeting WWC standards
- the role of effect sizes in tier determinations and prioritizing which interventions educators should select.

A final issue is determining how to assess the "totality" or "body of evidence" for an intervention more formally. For example, according to a strict interpretation of current guidance, one statistically significant negative result—even if the effect size is very small or even meaningless in practice—could counter a body of evidence with numerous statistically significant positive results with practically important effect sizes. Conversely, a study can meet the highest tier with only one statistically significant positive result, even if that finding does not have a practically important effect size or the study has numerous nonsignificant findings. Moreover, because research practices known to increase false positive rates (e.g., analyzing an outcome numerous ways and reporting only a selected subset of these analyses) are common in social intervention research, it is possible that a single statistically significant effect is an incorrect rejection of the null hypothesis (i.e., claiming there is an effect when there actually is no effect).

APPENDIX B

Summary of Evidence Table

The nonregulatory guidance from the U.S. Department of Education recommends that SEAs, LEAs, districts, schools, and other stakeholders select relevant, evidence-based interventions that best serve the needs identified in their needs assessments. This appendix provides a brief snapshot of the evidence we found for each evidence-based SEL intervention, while the detailed intervention summaries in our companion volume provide a more extensive overview of each intervention (Grant et al., 2017). From the nonregulatory guidance, we recommend that educators use Table B.1 to guide the selection of relevant, evidence-based interventions:

1. Start at the top of the table and work downward. The table is organized by strength of the evidence for making causal inference according to the nonregulatory guidance, and the nonregulatory guidance recommends prioritizing these interventions because inferences that the intervention led to positive effects are more likely to be true.
2. Find the interventions that have positive results for outcomes in the domains identified in a needs assessment as the biggest priorities.
3. Among interventions addressing priority outcome domains, identify those that have been validated in settings and populations similar to the one being served.
4. Among interventions addressing priority outcome domains with relevant settings and populations, identify those that are feasible

with LEAs' local capacities by assessing the implementers of the interventions and key intervention components.

5. Use the detailed intervention summaries in our companion volume for further information on the highest tier of interventions that are locally feasible and address local priority outcomes, settings, and populations to guide ultimate intervention selection and implementation.
6. Among interventions reaching this stage, consider prioritizing those with larger effects on measures of interest and that are likely to be acceptable—particularly to the students being served.[1]
   a. It is important to reiterate that stakeholders consider not just the outcome domain, but the *specific* measures *within priority outcome domains* to ensure that evidence of effect matches the precise constructs of interest.

---

[1] We caution against a deterministic use of effect sizes in intervention selection (i.e., always selecting the intervention with larger effect sizes). Reasons other than the effectiveness of an intervention can cause effect sizes to differ across studies (e.g., differing severity of social and emotional deficits among students at baseline). Instead, we have recommended considering effect sizes only after prioritizing the (1) quality of a study for making causal inferences, (2) beneficial effects on priority outcome domains, (3) similarity of study context to context of interest, and (4) feasibility of implementation in context of interest.

Table B.1
Summary of Evidence

Intervention	Sample	Positive Results (Tier)	Special Populations	Implementers	Key Intervention Components
Second Step (4 studies)	16,858 students 14+ sites Grades K–8	2 Intrapersonal outcomes (I): hyperactivity, learning skills 4 Interpersonal outcomes: antisocial behavior (III), conduct problems (I), physical aggression (I), social competence (III) 1 Academic attainment outcome (III): absences	Racial/ethnic minority Low SES Urban/ suburban/ rural	Teachers	• Classroom curriculum • Professional development • Implementation support • Website
Playworks (1 study)	2,331 students 6 sites Grades 4–5	3 Intrapersonal outcomes (I): class readiness, on-task behavior, transitioning from recess to learning 5 Climate/safety outcomes (I): bullying, inclusiveness, student ownership of recess activities, student safety, student use of positive language	Racial/ethnic minority Low SES Urban	Teachers Support staff	• Classroom curriculum • Applications outside the classroom • Out-of-school time • Website
Tools for Getting Along (2 studies)	4,118 students 4+ sites Grades 4–5	2 Intrapersonal outcomes (III): anger control, trait anger 3 Interpersonal outcomes (I): orientation to problem solving, rational problem solving, social problem solving	Low SES	Teachers Counselors	• Classroom curriculum • Professional development • Implementation support • Website

Table B.1—Continued

Intervention	Sample	Positive Results (Tier)	Special Populations	Implementers	Key Intervention Components
We Have Skills! (1 study)	1,661 students 4+ sites Grades K–3	1 Interpersonal outcome (I): social skills	Racial/ethnic minority Low SES	Teachers	• Classroom curriculum • Changing the learning environment • Family/community involvement • Professional development • Implementation support • Website
Connect with Kids (1 study)	352 students 4 sites Grades 7–12	1 Intrapersonal outcome (II): intrapersonal character traits 1 Civic outcome (II): civic character traits 1 Climate/safety outcome (II): perceived character of classmates	Urban/ suburban/ rural	Teachers	• Classroom curriculum • Family/community involvement • Professional development • Implementation support • Website
Class-Wide Function-Related Intervention Teams (1 study)	2,862+ students 3 sites Grades K–5	1 Intrapersonal outcome (I): on-task behavior	Racial/ethnic minority Low SES Urban	Teachers	• Classroom curriculum • Changing the learning environment • Professional development • Implementation support

Table B.1—Continued

Intervention	Sample	Positive Results (Tier)	Special Populations	Implementers	Key Intervention Components
Michigan Model for Health (1 study)	3,383 students 2+ sites Grades 4–5	3 Interpersonal outcomes (I): aggressive behavior, interpersonal communication, social and emotional skills	Low SES Urban/ suburban/ rural	Teachers	• Classroom curriculum • Professional development • Implementation support • Website
Positive Action (4 studies)	5,670 students 5 sites Grades 1–8	6 Intrapersonal outcomes (III): academic behaviors, academic motivation, disaffection with learning, self-concept, self-control, self-esteem 7 Interpersonal outcomes (III): aggressive problem solving, beliefs supportive of aggression, conduct problems, deviant peer affiliation, prosocial interactions, prosocial peer affiliation, social-emotional skills 2 Academic achievement outcomes (II): mathematics, reading 2 Academic attainment outcomes: absences (I), retention (III) 2 Disciplinary outcomes: suspensions (I), referrals (III) 2 Civic outcomes (III): honesty, morality	Racial/ethnic minority Low SES Urban/rural	Teachers Counselors Administrators	• Classroom curriculum • Changing the learning environment • Applications outside the classroom • Family/community involvement • Professional development • Implementation support • Website

Table B.1—Continued

Intervention	Sample	Positive Results (Tier)	Special Populations	Implementers	Key Intervention Components
Positive Action (continued)		3 Climate/safety outcomes (III): bullying behaviors, student safety and well-being, verbal and physical harassment at school			
Steps to Respect (2 studies)	4,066 students 5 sites Grades 3–6	5 Interpersonal outcomes: agreeable social interactions (I), argumentative social interactions (I), assertiveness (I), nonbullying aggression (I), social competency (III) 9 Climate/safety outcomes: acceptance of bullying (I), bullying (I/III), bullying encouragement (I), bystander responsibility (I/III), exclusionary gossip (I), staff responsiveness to bullying (I/III), student responsiveness to bullying (III), student climate (III), target of bullying (I)	Low SES Urban/ suburban/ rural	Teachers Counselors Administrators Support staff	• Classroom curriculum • Applications outside the classroom • Family/community involvement • Professional development • Implementation support • Website

Table B.1—Continued

Intervention	Sample	Positive Results (Tier)	Special Populations	Implementers	Key Intervention Components
Social Skills Improvement System—Classwide Intervention Program (1 study)	494 students 2 sites Grade 2	5 Intrapersonal outcomes (I): academic motivation, academic engagement, classroom engagement, responsibility, self-control 4 Interpersonal outcomes (I): communication, cooperation, empathy, social skills 1 Climate/safety outcome (I): disruptive classroom environment	Urban/rural	Teachers	• Classroom curriculum • Professional development • Implementation support • Website
Too Good for Violence (1 study)	999 students 1 site Grade 3	1 Intrapersonal outcome (III): emotional competency 6 Interpersonal outcomes (III): communication skills, inappropriate social behavior, prosocial behavior, resistance skills, social adaptability, social skills	Racial/ethnic minority Low SES Urban/suburban/rural	Teachers Support staff	• Classroom curriculum • Changing the learning environment • Implementation support • Website
Raising Healthy Children (1 study)	938 students 1+ sites Grades 1–2	1 Intrapersonal outcome (III): commitment to school 2 Interpersonal outcomes (III): antisocial behavior, social competency	Suburban	Teachers Support staff	• Changing the learning environment • Out-of-school time • Family/community involvement • Professional development • Implementation support • Website

Table B.1—Continued

Intervention	Sample	Positive Results (Tier)	Special Populations	Implementers	Key Intervention Components
Building Assets—Reducing Risks (1 study)	555 students 1 site Grade 9	2 Academic achievement outcomes (III): mathematics, reading 2 Academic attainment outcomes (III): no failed course credits, number of core course credits	Low SES Suburban	Teachers Counselors Administrators Support staff	• Classroom curriculum • Changing the learning environment • Applications outside the classroom • Family/community involvement • Professional development • Implementation support • Website
Mindfulness Training (3 studies)	646 students 3 sites Grades 1–3, 5–8	5 Intrapersonal outcomes (III): attention, selective attention, self-hostility, test anxiety, working memory capacity 3 Interpersonal outcomes (III): negative social coping strategies, rumination to cope with social situations, social skills	Racial/ethnic minority Low SES Urban	Support staff	• Classroom curriculum • Implementation support

Table B.1—Continued

Intervention	Sample	Positive Results (Tier)	Special Populations	Implementers	Key Intervention Components
PATHS (4 studies)	5,428 students 11 sites Grades 1–6	2 Intrapersonal outcomes (III): cognitive concentration, cognitive regulation 7 Interpersonal outcomes (III): aggressive interpersonal negotiation strategies, aggressive social problem solving, authority acceptance, conduct problems, hostile attribution bias, problem behaviors, social competence 3 Academic achievement outcomes (III): mathematics, reading, writing	Racial/ethnic minority Low SES Urban/ suburban/ rural	Teachers Administrators Support staff	• Classroom curriculum • Changing the learning environment • Applications outside the classroom • Family/community involvement • Professional development • Implementation support • Website
Take the Lead (1 study)	323 students 1 site Grade 7	2 Climate/safety outcomes (III): bullying, victimization	Suburban	Teachers	• Classroom curriculum • Family/community involvement • Professional development
PRAISE (1 study)	290 students 1 site Grades 3–4	1 Interpersonal outcome (III): social problem solving	Racial/ethnic minority Low SES Urban	Teachers Counselors	• Classroom curriculum • Implementation support

Table B.1—Continued

Intervention	Sample	Positive Results (Tier)	Special Populations	Implementers	Key Intervention Components
School-to-Jobs (1 study)	264 students 1 site Grade 8	2 Intrapersonal outcomes (III): academic mindset, initiative taking 1 Academic achievement outcome (III): standardized tests passed 1 Academic attainment outcome (III): absences	Racial/ethnic minority Low SES Urban	Support staff	• Classroom curriculum • Family/community involvement • Professional development • Implementation support
Ready to Learn (1 study)	260 students 1+ sites Grade K	1 Intrapersonal outcome (III): listening comprehension 1 Interpersonal outcome (III): behavior	Suburban	Teachers	• Classroom curriculum • Changing the learning environment • Professional development • Implementation support
Student Success Skills (2 studies)	529 students 2 sites Grades 5, 7	3 Intrapersonal outcomes (III): cognitive regulation, emotion control, self-awareness 1 Interpersonal outcome (III): prosocial behavior 2 Academic achievement outcomes (III): mathematics, reading 3 Climate/safety outcomes (III): bullying, class climate, classmate support	Racial/ethnic minority Low SES Suburban	Teachers Counselors	• Classroom curriculum • Changing the learning environment • Professional development • Implementation support • Website

Table B.1—Continued

Intervention	Sample	Positive Results (Tier)	Special Populations	Implementers	Key Intervention Components
Yoga (7 studies)	800 students 7 sites Grades 4–6 9 11–12	7 Intrapersonal outcomes (III): anger control, coping skills, emotional regulation, resilience, school engagement, self-regulation, stress management 1 Academic attainment outcome (III): absences 1 Disciplinary outcome (III): detention	Racial/ethnic minority Low SES Urban/rural	Teachers Support staff	• Classroom curriculum • Changing the learning environment • Out-of-school time • Professional development • Implementation support • Website
Social Aggression Prevention Program (1 study)	134 students 1 site Grades 4–6	1 Interpersonal outcome (III): social problem-solving skills	Racial/ethnic minority Urban	Counselors	• Classroom curriculum • Professional development • Implementation support
Go Grrrls (2 studies)	173 students 2 sites Grade 7	2 Intrapersonal outcomes (III): self-esteem, self-efficacy 2 Interpersonal outcomes (III): assertiveness, friendship esteem	Urban/ suburban	Counselors	• Classroom curriculum • Professional development • Implementation support • Website

Table B.1—Continued

Intervention	Sample	Positive Results (Tier)	Special Populations	Implementers	Key Intervention Components
Conflict Resolution and Peer Mediation (1 study)	92 students 1 site Grade 9	2 Interpersonal outcomes (III): attitudes toward conflict resolution, negotiation skills	Suburban	Teachers	• Classroom curriculum • Implementation support
Mental Contrasting with Implementation Intentions (1 study)	77 students 1 site Grade 5	1 Intrapersonal outcome (III): preparedness for school 1 Academic attainment outcome (III): attendance	Racial/ethnic minority Low SES Urban	Support staff	• Classroom curriculum
Tools of the Mind (1 study)	759 students 12 sites Grade K	3 Intrapersonal outcomes (III): cognitive flexibility, inhibitory control, working memory 3 Academic achievement outcomes (III): mathematics, reading, vocabulary	Low SES	Teachers Support staff	• Changing the learning environment • Professional development • Implementation support • Website

Table B.1—Continued

Intervention	Sample	Positive Results (Tier)	Special Populations	Implementers	Key Intervention Components
INSIGHTS (2 studies)	583 students 4 sites Grades K–2	1 Intrapersonal outcome (III): attention 2 Interpersonal outcomes (III): behavior problems at home, behavior problems at school 2 Academic achievement outcomes (III): mathematics, reading 1 Climate/safety outcome (III): classroom emotional support	Racial/ethnic minority Low SES Urban	Teachers Counselors Support staff	• Classroom curriculum • Changing the learning environment • Family/community involvement • Professional development • Implementation support • Website
Success for Kids (1 study)	737 students 3 sites Grades 1–8	3 Intrapersonal outcomes (III): hyperactivity, self-esteem, study skills 5 Interpersonal outcomes (III): behavioral problems, communication, externalizing problems, social adaptability, social skills 1 Disciplinary outcome (III): school problems 1 Civic outcome (III): leadership competencies	Racial/ethnic minority Low SES	Teachers Support staff	• Classroom curriculum • Out-of-school time • Professional development • Implementation support • Website

Table B.1—Continued

Intervention	Sample	Positive Results (Tier)	Special Populations	Implementers	Key Intervention Components
Bullying Literature Project (1 study)	168 students 2 sites Grades 3–4	1 Interpersonal outcome (III): prosocial behavior	Racial/ethnic minority Low SES	Teachers Counselors	• Classroom curriculum • Applications outside the classroom • Family/community involvement • Professional development • Implementation support
4Rs (1 study)	1,184 students 1 site Grades 3–4	3 Interpersonal outcomes (III): aggressive behavior, hostile attribution bias, socially competent behavior	Racial/ethnic minority Low SES Urban	Teachers	• Classroom curriculum • Changing the learning environment • Professional development • Implementation support • Website
School/ Community Intervention (1 study)	1,153 students 1+ sites Grades 5–8	2 Interpersonal outcomes (III): provoking behavior, violent behavior 1 Disciplinary outcome (III): school delinquency	Racial/ethnic minority Low SES Urban	Counselors	• Classroom curriculum • Applications outside the classroom • Family/community involvement • Professional development • Implementation support • Website

Table B.1—Continued

Intervention	Sample	Positive Results (Tier)	Special Populations	Implementers	Key Intervention Components
Social Development Curriculum (1 study)	1,153 students 1+ sites Grades 5–8	1 Interpersonal outcome (III): violent behavior	Racial/ethnic minority Low SES Urban	Counselors	• Classroom curriculum • Professional development • Implementation support • Website
Youth Matters (1 study)	1,126 students 1 site Grades 4–5	1 Climate/safety outcome (III): victimization	Racial/ethnic minority Urban	Support staff	• Classroom curriculum • Changing the learning environment • Applications outside the classroom • Professional development • Implementation support
Friend to Friend (1 study)	665 students 1 site Grades 3–5	1 Interpersonal outcome (III): prosocial behavior 1 Climate/safety outcome (III): student-teacher relationships	Racial/ethnic minority Low SES Urban	Teachers Counselors Support staff	• Classroom curriculum • Applications outside the classroom • Implementation support

Table B.1—Continued

Intervention	Sample	Positive Results (Tier)	Special Populations	Implementers	Key Intervention Components
Responding in Peaceful and Positive Ways (3 studies)	2,167 students 7 sites Grades 6–7	6 Interpersonal outcomes (III): aggressive behavior, approval of nonviolent behavior, delinquent behavior, disapproval of violent behavior, nonviolent problem solving, physical aggression 1 Disciplinary outcome (III): disciplinary code violations for violence 3 Climate/safety outcomes (III): peer provocations, peer support for prosocial behavior, victimization and harassment	Racial/ethnic minority Low SES Urban/rural	Support staff	• Classroom curriculum • Professional development • Implementation support
Real Lives (1 study)	323 students 1+ sites Grades 9–10	3 Civic outcomes (III): ethnocultural empathy, interest in current events, interest in other countries	Racial/ethnic minority Urban/ suburban	Teachers Support staff	• Classroom curriculum
KnowConflict (1 study)	198 students 1 site Grade 9	1 Interpersonal outcome (III): attitudes toward violence	Urban	Teachers	• Classroom curriculum

Table B.1—Continued

Intervention	Sample	Positive Results (Tier)	Special Populations	Implementers	Key Intervention Components
Good Behavior Game (1 study)	949 students 6 sites Grades 1–3	2 Academic achievement outcomes (III): mathematics, reading	Urban/ suburban/ rural Low SES	Teachers	• Changing the learning environment • Family/community involvement • Professional development • Implementation support • Website
Resolving Conflict Creatively Program (1 study)	11,160 students 4 sites Grades 1–6	6 Interpersonal outcomes (III): aggressive behavior, aggressive interpersonal negotiation strategies, competent interpersonal negotiation strategies, conduct problems, hostile attribution bias, prosocial behavior	Racial/ethnic minority Low SES Urban	Teachers Administrators	• Classroom curriculum • Changing the learning environment • Applications outside the classroom • Family/community involvement • Professional development • Implementation support • Website
Responsive Classroom (2 studies)	5,694 students 2 sites Grades 2–5	2 Interpersonal outcomes (III): assertion, prosocial behavior 2 Academic achievement outcomes (III): mathematics, reading	Racial/ethnic minority Urban	Teachers Administrators	• Changing the learning environment • Applications outside the classroom • Professional development • Implementation support • Website

Table B.1—Continued

Intervention	Sample	Positive Results (Tier)	Special Populations	Implementers	Key Intervention Components
Bully-Proofing Your School (1 study)	3,497 students 2+ sites Grades 3–5	2 Interpersonal outcomes (III): physical aggression perpetration, relational aggression perpetration 5 Climate/safety outcomes (III): physical aggression victimization, relational aggression victimization, witnessing aggression, discouragement of bullying at school, perceived school safety	Racial/ethnic minority Low SES	Teachers Counselors	• Classroom curriculum • Changing the learning environment • Applications outside the classroom • Family/community involvement • Professional development • Implementation support • Website
Open Circle (1 study)	154 students 2 sites Grade 4	2 Interpersonal outcomes (III): problem behavior, social skills	Urban/ suburban	Teachers Counselors Administrators Support staff	• Classroom curriculum • Changing the learning environment • Family/community involvement • Implementation support • Website

Table B.1—Continued

Intervention	Sample	Positive Results (Tier)	Special Populations	Implementers	Key Intervention Components
Olweus Bullying Prevention Program (1 study)	6,518 students 1+ sites Grades 6–8	1 Climate/safety outcome (III): perception that others will intervene	Racial/ethnic minority Low SES	Teachers Counselors Administrators Support staff	• Classroom curriculum • Changing the learning environment • Applications outside the classroom • Family/community involvement • Professional development • Implementation support • Website
Caring School Communities (1 study)	3,098 students 1 site Grades 3–5	3 Climate/safety outcomes (III): classroom supportiveness, student autonomy, trust in students	Low SES	Teachers Administrators Support staff	• Classroom curriculum • Changing the learning environment • Applications outside the classroom • Out-of-school time • Family/community involvement • Professional development • Implementation support • Website

Table B.1—Continued

Intervention	Sample	Positive Results (Tier)	Special Populations	Implementers	Key Intervention Components
Peacemakers (1 study)	1,822 students 1 site Grades 4–8	1 Interpersonal outcome (III): aggressive behavior 3 Disciplinary outcomes (III): disciplinary incidents for aggressive behavior, referral to conflict mediation, suspensions	Racial/ethnic minority Low SES Urban	Teachers Counselors Administrators	• Classroom curriculum • Changing the learning environment • Applications outside the classroom • Professional development • Implementation support
Violence Prevention Project (1 study)	1,112 students 1 site Grades 9–10	1 Intrapersonal outcome (III): academic self-concept 1 Interpersonal outcome (III): conflict resolution strategies	Racial/ethnic minority Low SES Urban	Teachers Administrators Support staff	• Classroom curriculum • Professional development • Implementation support • Website
Going for the Goal (1 study)	479 students 1 site Grade 7	1 Intrapersonal outcome (III): self-control 1 Interpersonal outcome (III): social problem-solving skills	Racial/ethnic minority Low SES Urban	Support staff	• Classroom curriculum • Professional development • Implementation support

Table B.1—Continued

Intervention	Sample	Positive Results (Tier)	Special Populations	Implementers	Key Intervention Components
Skills for Growing (1 study)	474 students 1 site Grades 3–5	1 Interpersonal outcome (III): relationship skills 1 Disciplinary outcome (III): minimally disruptive behavior 1 Climate/safety outcome (III): safe and respectful climate	Low SES Urban	Teachers Counselors Administrators	• Classroom curriculum • Applications outside the classroom • Out-of-school time • Family/community involvement • Professional development • Implementation support • Website
I Can Problem Solve (1 study)	226 students 1 site Grades K–1	3 Interpersonal outcomes (III): prosocial behavior, overt aggression, relational aggression	Racial/ethnic minority Low SES Urban	Teachers	• Classroom curriculum • Changing the learning environment • Professional development • Implementation support • Website
Talking with TJ (1 study)	208 students 1 site Grade 3	1 Intrapersonal outcome (III): self-concept	Racial/ethnic minority Low SES Urban	Teachers Support staff	• Classroom curriculum • Changing the learning environment • Family/community involvement • Professional development • Implementation support • Website

Table B.1—Continued

Intervention	Sample	Positive Results (Tier)	Special Populations	Implementers	Key Intervention Components
Urban Improv (1 study)	140 students 1 site Grade 4	2 Intrapersonal outcomes (III): hyperactivity, self-control 2 Interpersonal outcomes (III): cooperative behavior, externalizing behavior	Racial/ethnic minority Urban	Support staff	• Classroom curriculum • Website
RAP Club (1 study)	49 students 1 site Grades 7–8	1 Intrapersonal outcome (III): emotional self-regulation 2 Interpersonal outcomes (III): authority acceptance, social competence	Racial/ethnic minority Low SES Urban	Counselors Support staff	• Classroom curriculum • Professional development • Implementation support
RULER (1 study)	273 students 1+ sites Grades 5–6	1 Intrapersonal outcome (III): school problems 1 Interpersonal outcome (III): social adaptability	Not applicable	Teachers	• Classroom curriculum • Professional development • Implementation support • Website
Strong Kids (1 study)	108 students 1 site Grades 3–4	1 Intrapersonal outcome (III): emotional competencies/assets 2 Interpersonal outcomes (III): social coping skills, social functioning	Not applicable	Teachers	• Classroom curriculum • Changing the learning environment • Professional development • Implementation support • Website

Table B.1—Continued

Intervention	Sample	Positive Results (Tier)	Special Populations	Implementers	Key Intervention Components
Making Choices (2 studies)	649 students 2 sites Grade 3	1 Intrapersonal outcome (III): cognitive concentration 9 Interpersonal outcomes (III): encoding social information, hostile attribution, overt aggression, peer acceptance, prosocial goal formulation, responsible decisionmaking, social aggression, social competence, social contact	Rural	Teachers Counselors	• Classroom curriculum • Changing the learning environment • Professional development • Implementation support • Website
Taekwondo (1 study)	46 students 1 site Grades 7–8	1 Intrapersonal outcome (III): behavior control	Racial/ethnic minority Low SES	Teachers	• Classroom curriculum
Project WIN (1 study)	34 students 1 site Grade 5	1 Interpersonal outcome (III): conflict resolution skills	Racial/ethnic minority Low SES Urban	Counselors	• Classroom curriculum • Changing the learning environment • Implementation support

Table B.1—Continued

Intervention	Sample	Positive Results (Tier)	Special Populations	Implementers	Key Intervention Components
Promoting Positive Peer Relationships (1 study)	636 students 1 site Grades 7–8	2 Climate/safety outcomes (III): attitudes toward bullying, peer supports against bullying	Racial/ethnic minority Suburban	Teachers	• Classroom curriculum • Professional development • Implementation support • Website
Quiet Time (1 study)	195 students 1 site Grade 9	1 Intrapersonal outcome (III): resilience	Racial/ethnic minority Urban	Teachers Support staff	• Classroom curriculum • Website
Competent Kids, Caring Communities (1 study)	119 students 1 site Grades 4–5	3 Intrapersonal outcomes (III): self-efficacy, attention/concentration, compliance 3 Interpersonal outcomes (III): prosocial problem-solving skills, social/emotional competence, aggression	Racial/ethnic minority Low SES Urban	Teachers	• Classroom curriculum • Changing the learning environment • Applications outside the classroom • Professional development • Implementation support • Website

Abbreviations

CASEL	Collaborative for Academic, Social, and Emotional Learning
EDGAR	Education Department General Administrative Regulations
ERIC	Education Resources Information Center
ESSA	Every Student Succeeds Act
IES	Institute of Education Sciences
K	kindergarten
LEA	local education agency
NRC	National Research Council
REL	Regional Education Laboratory
RCT	randomized-control trial
SEA	state education agency
SEL	social and emotional learning
SES	socioeconomic status
WWC	What Works Clearinghouse

Bibliography

Aber, J. Lawrence, Joshua L. Brown, and Stephanie M. Jones, "Developmental Trajectories Toward Violence in Middle Childhood: Course, Demographic Differences, and Response to School-Based Intervention," *Developmental Psychology*, Vol. 39, No. 2, March 2003, pp. 324–348.

Abry, Tashia, Chris A. Hulleman, and Sara E. Rimm-Kaufman, "Using Indices of Fidelity to Intervention Core Components to Identify Program Active Ingredients," *American Journal of Evaluation*, Vol. 36, No. 3, September 2015, pp. 320–338.

Abry, Tashia, Sara E. Rimm-Kaufman, Ross A. Larsen, and Alexis J. Brewer, "The Influence of Fidelity of Implementation on Teacher–Student Interaction Quality in the Context of a Randomized Controlled Trial of the Responsive Classroom Approach," *Journal of School Psychology*, Vol. 51, No. 4, August 2013, pp. 437–453.

Ackerman Institute for the Family, "Competent Kids, Caring Communities," website, undated. As of October 19, 2017:
http://www.competentkids.org

Advocates for Youth, "Aban Aya Youth Project," webpage, 2008. As of October 23, 2017:
http://www.advocatesforyouth.org/publications/publications-a-z/2112-aban-aya-youth-project

AEM Corporation, "Synthesis of Information on Evidence-Based Practices for School Improvement: 20 Studies and Tools Focused on Evidence-Based Practices in School Improvement," Herndon, Va., December 2016. As of March 13, 2017:
http://ssn.airprojects.org/Synthesis_of_Evidence_Resources.pdf

Alonso-Coello, Pablo, Andrew D. Oxman, Jenny Moberg, Romina Brignardello-Petersen, Elie A. Akl, Marina Davoli, Shaun Treweek, Reem A. Mustafa, Per O. Vandvik, Joerg Meerpohl, Gordon H. Guyatt, and Holger J. Schünemann, "GRADE Evidence to Decision (EtD) frameworks: A Systematic and Transparent Approach to Making Well Informed Healthcare Choices. 2: Clinical Practice Guidelines," *BMJ*, Vol. 353, i2089, June 30, 2016a.

Alonso-Coello, Pablo, Holger J. Schünemann, Jenny Moberg, Romina Brignardello-Petersen, Elie A. Akl, Marina Davoli, Shaun Treweek, Reem A. Mustafa, Gabriel Rada, Sarah Rosenbaum, Angela Morelli, Gordon H. Guyatt, and Andrew D. Oxman, "GRADE Evidence to Decision (EtD) Frameworks: A Systematic and Transparent Approach to Making Well Informed Healthcare Choices. 1: Introduction," *BMJ*, Vol. 353, i2016, June 28, 2016b.

Aragon, Stephanie, Mike Griffith, Micah Ann Wixom, Julie Woods, and Emily Workman "ESSA: Quick Guides on Top Issues," Education Commission of the States, Denver, Colo., 2016. As of October 111, 2017: https://www.ecs.org/ec-content/uploads/ESSA-Quick-guides-on-top-issues.pdf

Bachen, Christine M., Pedro F. Hernández-Ramos, and Chad Raphael, "Simulating REAL LIVES: Promoting Global Empathy and Interest in Learning through Simulation Games," *Simulation & Gaming*, Vol. 43, No. 4, August 2012, pp. 437–460.

Bachen, Christine M., Pedro F. Hernández-Ramos, Chad Raphael, and Amanda Waldron, "Civic Play and Civic Gaps: Can Life Simulation Games Advance Educational Equity?" *Journal of Information Technology and Politics*, Vol. 12, 2015, pp. 378–395.

Bacon, Tina P., *The Effects of the Too Good for Violence Prevention Program on Student Behaviors and Protective Factors*, Tampa, Fla.: Mendez Foundation, 2003.

Bauer, Nerissa S., Paula Lozano, and Frederick P. Rivara, "The Effectiveness of the Olweus Bullying Prevention Program in Public Middle Schools: A Controlled Trial," *Journal of Adolescent Health*, Vol. 40, No. 3, March 2007, pp. 266–274.

Bavarian, Niloofar, Kendra M. Lewis, David L. DuBois, Alan Acock, Samuel Vuchinich, Naida Silverthorn, and Brian R. Flay, "Using Social-Emotional and Character Development to Improve Academic Outcomes: A Matched-Pair, Cluster-Randomized Controlled Trial in Low-Income, Urban Schools," *Journal of School Health*, Vol. 83, No. 11, November 2013, pp. 771–779.

Beets, Michael W., Brian R. Flay, Samuel Vuchinich, Frank J. Snyder, Alan Acock, Kin-Kit Li, Kate Burns, Isaac J. Washburn, and Joseph Durlak, "Use of a Social and Character Development Program to Prevent Substance Use, Violent Behaviors, and Sexual Activity Among Elementary-School Students in Hawaii," *American Journal of Public Health*, Vol. 99, No. 8, August 2009, pp. 1438–1445.

Bergen-Cico, Dessa, Rachel Razza, and Amy Timmins, "Fostering Self-Regulation Through Curriculum Infusion of Mindful Yoga: A Pilot Study of Efficacy and Feasibility," *Journal of Child and Family Studies*, Vol. 24, No. 11, November 2015, pp. 3448–3461.

Beyler, Nicholas, Martha Bleeker, Susanne James-Burdumy, Jane Fortson, Rebecca A. London, Lisa Westrich, Katie Stokes-Guinan, and Sebastian Castrechini, *Findings from an Experimental Evaluation of Playworks: Effects on Play, Physical Activity, and Recess*, Princeton, N.J.: Mathematica Policy Research, 2013.

Bierman, Karen L., John D. Coie, Kenneth A. Dodge, Mark T. Greenberg, John E. Lochman, Robert J. McMahon, and Ellen Pinderhughes, "The Effects of a Multiyear Universal Social-Emotional Learning Program: The Role of Student and School Characteristics," *Journal of Consulting and Clinical Psychology*, Vol. 78, No. 2, April 2010, pp. 156–168.

Blair, Clancy, and C. Cybele Raver, "Closing the Achievement Gap Through Modification of Neurocognitive and Neuroendocrine Function: Results from a Cluster Randomized Controlled Trial of an Innovative Approach to the Education of Children in Kindergarten," *PLoS ONE*, Vol. 9, No. 11, November 12, 2014.

Bleeker, Martha, Susanne James-Burdumy, Nicholas Beyler, Allison Hedley Dodd, Rebecca A. London, Lisa Westrich, Katie Stokes-Guinan, and Sebastian Castrechini, *Findings from a Randomized Experiment of Playworks: Selected Results from Cohort 1*, Princeton, N.J.: Mathematica Policy Research, 2012.

Bohnert, Amy M., and Amanda K. Ward, "Making a Difference: Evaluating the Girls in the Game (GIG) After-School Program," *Journal of Early Adolescence*, Vol. 33, No. 1, January 2013, pp. 104–130.

Boyle, Douglas, and Connie Hassett-Walker, "Reducing Overt and Relational Aggression Among Young Children: The Results from a Two-Year Outcome Evaluation," *Journal of School Violence*, Vol. 7, No. 1, February 2008, pp. 27–42.

Brackett, Marc A., Susan E. Rivers, Maria R. Reyes, and Peter Salovey, "Enhancing Academic Performance and Social and Emotional Competence with the RULER Feeling Words Curriculum," *Learning & Individual Differences*, Vol. 22, No. 2, April 2012, pp. 218–224.

Brigman, Greg A., and Linda D. Webb, "Ready to Learn: Teaching Kindergarten Students School Success Skills," *Journal of Educational Research*, Vol. 96, No. 5, May 2003, pp. 286–292.

Brown, Eric C., Sabrina Low, Brian H. Smith, and Kevin P. Haggerty, "Outcomes from a School-Randomized Controlled Trial of Steps to Respect: A Bullying Prevention Program," *School Psychology Review*, Vol. 40, No. 3, September 2011, pp. 423–433.

Brown, Joshua L., Stephanie M. Jones, Maria D. LaRusso, and J. Lawrence Aber, "Improving Classroom Quality: Teacher Influences and Experimental Impacts of the 4Rs Program," *Journal of Educational Psychology*, Vol. 102, No. 1, February 2010, pp. 153–167.

Building Assets, Reducing Risks, "BARR," website, undated. As of October 19, 2017: http://www.barrcenter.org

Cappella, Elise, Erin E. O'Connor, Meghan P. McCormick, Ashley R. Turbeville, Ashleigh J. Collins, and Sandee G. McClowry, "Classwide Efficacy of INSIGHTS: Observed Teacher Practices and Student Behaviors in Kindergarten and First Grade," *Elementary School Journal*, Vol. 116, No. 2, December 2015, pp. 217–241.

Cappella, E., and R. Weinstein, "The Prevention of Social Aggression Among Girls," *Social Development*, Vol. 15, No. 3, August 2006, pp. 434–462.

CASEL—*See* Collaborative for Academic, Social, and Emotional Learning.

Catalano, Richard F., James J. Mazza, Tracy W. Harrachi, Robert D. Abbott, Kevin P. Haggerty, and Charles B. Fleming, "Raising Healthy Children Through Enhancing Social Development in Elementary School: Results After 1.5 Years," *Journal of School Psychology*, Vol. 41, No. 2, April 2003, pp. 143–164.

Center for the Collaborative Classroom, "Caring School Community," webpage, undated. As of October 19, 2017:
https://www.collaborativeclassroom.org/caring-school-community

Center for Community Health and Development, "Developing a Logic Model or Theory of Change," Community Tool Box website, Lawrence, Kan.: University of Kansas, 2017. As of July 31, 2017:
http://ctb.ku.edu/en/table-of-contents/overview/models-for-community-health-and-development/logic-model-development/main

Center for Research and Reform in Education, "Evidence for ESSA," webpage, Johns Hopkins University, 2017. As of March 10, 2017:
http://www.evidenceforessa.org/

Center for Schools and Communities, "I Can Problem Solve," website, undated. As of October 19, 2017:
http://www.icanproblemsolve.info

Chang, Florence, and Marco A. Muñoz, "School Personnel Educating the Whole Child: Impact of Character Education on Teachers' Self-Assessment and Student Development," *Journal of Personnel Evaluation in Education*, Vol. 19, No. 1–2, June 2006, pp. 35–49.

Chiefs for Change, "ESSA and Evidence: Why It Matters," policy brief, July 2016a. As of March 13, 2017:
http://chiefsforchange.org/wp-content/uploads/2016/07/ESSA-and-Evidence-Why-It-Matters.pdf

———, *ESSA Indicators: Indicators of School Quality and Student Success*, October 16, 2016b. As of March 16, 2017:
http://chiefsforchange.org/policy-paper/3244/

Code of Federal Regulations, Title 34, Section 77.1, Definitions that Apply to Department Regulations, January 20, 2015.

Collaborative for Academic, Social, and Emotional Learning, *2013 CASEL Guide: Effective Social and Emotional Learning Programs: Preschool and Elementary School Edition*, Chicago, Ill., 2013.

———, *2015 CASEL Guide: Effective Social and Emotional Learning Programs: Middle and High School Edition*, Chicago, Ill., 2015.

———, "Core SEL Competencies," webpage, 2016. As of March 15, 2017: http://www.casel.org/core-competencies/

———, "Identifying K–12 Standards for SEL in All 50 States," table, February 2017. As of March 13, 2017:
http://www.casel.org/wp-content/uploads/2017/02/K-12StandardsforSELinallStates-Feb2017.pdf

Committee for Children, "Previous Program Resources," webpage, undated. As of October 23, 2017:
http://www.cfchildren.org/resources/previous-programs/

———, "Second Step," website, undated. As of October 23, 2017:
http://www.secondstep.org/

Conley, David T., "Rethinking the Notion of 'Noncognitive,'" *Education Weekly*, Vol. 32, No. 18, January 2013, pp. 20–21.

Connect with Kids Network, "Connect with Kids," website, undated. As of October 19, 2017:
https://connectwithkids.com

Corsello, Maryann, and Anu Sharma, *The Building Assets-Reducing Risks Program: Replication and Expansion of an Effective Strategy to Turn Around Low-Achieving Schools*, final report, October 2015. As of July 31, 2017:
http://files.eric.ed.gov/fulltext/ED560804.pdf

Crean, Hugh F., and Deborah B. Johnson, "Promoting Alternative Thinking Strategies (PATHS) and Elementary School Aged Children's Aggression: Results from a Cluster Randomized Trial," *American Journal of Community Psychology*, Vol. 52, No. 1–2, September 2013, pp. 56–72.

Daly, Leslie A., Sara C. Haden, Marshall Hagins, Nicholas Papouchis, and Paul Michael Ramirez, "Yoga and Emotion Regulation in High School Students: A Randomized Controlled Trial," *Evidence-Based Complementary and Alternative Medicine*, August 2015, pp. 1–8.

Daunic, Ann P., Stephen W. Smith, Cynthia W. Garvan, Brian R. Barber, Mallory K. Becker, Christine D. Peters, Gregory G. Taylor, Christopher L. Van Loan, Wei Li, and Arlene H. Naranjo, "Reducing Developmental Risk For Emotional/Behavioral Problems: A Randomized Controlled Trial Examining the Tools for Getting Along Curriculum," *Journal of School Psychology*, Vol. 50, No. 2, April 2012, pp. 149–166.

David Lynch Foundation, "The Quiet Time Program: Improving Academic Performance and Reducing Stress and Violence," webpage, undated. As of October 23, 2017:
https://www.davidlynchfoundation.org/schools.html

Dilworth, Janean E'guya, Kathariya Mokrue, and Maurice J. Elias, "The Efficacy of a Video-Based Teamwork-Building Series with Urban Elementary School Students: A Pilot Investigation," *Journal of School Psychology*, Vol. 40, No. 4, August 2002, pp. 329–346.

DiPerna, James Clyde, Puiwa Lei, Jillian Bellinger, and Weiyi Cheng, "Efficacy of the Social Skills Improvement System Classwide Intervention Program (SSIS-CIP) Primary Version," *School Psychology Quarterly*, Vol. 30, No. 1, March 2015, pp. 123–141.

———, "Effects of a Universal Positive Classroom Behavior Program on Student Learning," *Psychology in the Schools*, Vol. 53, No. 2, February 2016, pp. 189–203.

Domino, Meg, "Measuring the Impact of an Alternative Approach to School Bullying," *Journal of School Health*, Vol. 83, No. 6, June 2013, pp. 430–437.

Duckworth, Angela L., Teri A. Kirby, Anton Gollwitzer, and Gabriele Oettingen, "From Fantasy to Action Mental Contrasting with Implementation Intentions (MCII) Improves Academic Performance in Children," *Social Psychological and Personality Science*, Vol. 4, No. 6, November 2013, pp. 745–753.

Durlak, Joseph A., Celene E. Domitrovich, Roger P. Weissberg, and Thomas P. Gullotta, eds., *Handbook of Social and Emotional Learning: Research and Practice*, New York: Guilford Press, 2015.

Durlak, Joseph A., Roger P. Weissberg, Allison B. Dymnicki, Rebecca D. Taylor, and Kriston B. Schellinger, "The Impact of Enhancing Students' Social and Emotional Learning: A Meta-Analysis of School-Based Universal Interventions," *Child Development*, Vol. 82, No. 1, 2011, pp. 405–432.

Dusenbury, Linda, Sophia Calin, Celene Domitrovich, and Roger P. Weissberg, "What Does Evidence-Based Instruction in Social and Emotional Learning Actually Look Like in Practice?" brief, Chicago, Ill.: CASEL, October 2015.

EPPI-Centre, "EPPI-Reviewer 4," website, Social Science Research Unit of the UCL Institute of Education, University of London, UK, 2017. As of July 31, 2017: https://eppi.ioe.ac.uk/CMS/Default.aspx?alias=eppi.ioe.ac.uk/cms/er4&

Espelage, Dorothy L., Sabrina Low, Joshua R. Polanin, and Eric C. Brown, "The Impact of a Middle School Program to Reduce Aggression, Victimization, and Sexual Violence," *Journal of Adolescent Health*, Vol. 53, No. 2, August 2013, pp. 180–186.

———, "Clinical Trial of Second Step© Middle-School Program: Impact on Aggression & Victimization," *Journal of Applied Developmental Psychology*, Vol. 37, No. 1, 2015, pp. 52–63.

Espelage, Dorothy L., Sabrina Low, Mark J. Van Ryzin, and Joshua R. Polanin, "Clinical Trial of Second Step Middle School Program: Impact on Bullying, Cyberbullying, Homophobic Teasing, and Sexual Harassment Perpetration," *School Psychology Review*, Vol. 44, No. 4, December 2015, pp. 464–479.

Farrell, Albert D., "The Multisite Violence Prevention Project: Impact of a Universal School-Based Violence Prevention Program on Social-Cognitive Outcomes," *Prevention Science*, Vol. 9, No. 231, December 2008, pp. 231–244.

Farrell, Albert D., Aleta L. Meyer, Terri N. Sullivan, and Eva M. Kung, "Evaluation of the Responding in Peaceful and Positive Ways (RIPP) Seventh Grade Violence Prevention Curriculum," *Journal of Child and Family Studies*, Vol. 12, No. 1, March 2003, pp. 101–120.

Farrell, Albert D., Robert E. Valois, and Aleta L. Meyer, "Evaluation of the RIPP-6 Violence Prevention Program at a Rural Middle School," *American Journal of Health Education*, Vol. 33, No. 3, June 2002, pp. 167–172.

Farrell, Albert D., Robert F. Valois, Aleta L. Meyer, and Ritchie P. Tidwell, "Impact of the RIPP Violence Prevention Program on Rural Middle School Students," *Journal of Primary Prevention*, Vol. 24, No. 2, December 2003, pp. 143–167.

Farrington, Camille A., Melissa Roderick, Elaine Allensworth, Jenny Nagaoka, Tasha Seneca Keyes, David W. Johnson, and Nicole O. Beechum, *Teaching Adolescents to Become Learners: The Role of Noncognitive Factors in Shaping School Performance—A Critical Literature Review*, Chicago, Ill.: Consortium on Chicago School Research, 2012.

Fernandez, Melanie A., Jonathan S. Adelstein, Samantha P. Miller, Margaret J. Areizaga, Dylann C. Gold, Amanda L. Sanchez, Sara A. Rothschild, Emily Hirsch, and Omar G. Gudino, "Teacher-Child Interaction Training: A Pilot Study With Random Assignment," *Behavior Therapy*, Vol. 46, No. 4, July 2015, pp. 463–477.

Flannery, Daniel J., Alexander T. Vazsonyi, Albert K. Liau, Shenyang Guo, Kenneth E. Powell, Henry Atha, Wendy Vesterdal, and Dennis Embry, "Initial Behavior Outcomes for the Peacebuilders Universal School-Based Violence Prevention Program," *Developmental Psychology*, Vol. 39, No. 2, March 2003, pp. 292–308.

Flay, Brian R., and Carol G. Allred, "Long-Term Effects of the Positive Action® Program," *American Journal of Health Behavior*, Vol. 27, No. 1, May 2003, pp. S6–S21.

Flay, Brian R., Sally Graumlich, Eisuke Segawa, James L. Burns, and Michelle Y. Holliday, "Effects of 2 Prevention Programs on High-Risk Behaviors Among African American Youth: A Randomized Trial," *Archives of Pediatrics & Adolescent Medicine*, Vol. 158, No. 4, April 2004, pp. 377–384.

Fonagy, Peter, Stuart W. Twemlow, Eric M. Vernberg, Jennifer Mize Nelson, Edward J. Dill, Todd D. Little, and John A. Sargent, "A Cluster Randomized Controlled Trial of Child-Focused Psychiatric Consultation and a School Systems–Focused Intervention to Reduce Aggression," *Journal of Child Psychology and Psychiatry*, Vol. 50, No. 5, May 2009, pp. 607–616.

Fortson, Jane, Susanne James-Burdumy, Martha Bleeker, Nicholas Beyler, Rebecca A. London, Lisa Westrich, Katie Stokes-Guinan, and Sebastian Castrechini, *Impact and Implementation Findings from an Experimental Evaluation of Playworks: Effects on School Climate, Academic Learning, Student Social Skills and Behavior*, Princeton, N.J.: Mathematica Policy Research, 2013.

Frank, Jennifer L., Kimberly Kohler, Adam Peal, and Bidyut Bose, "Effectiveness of a School-Based Yoga Program on Adolescent Mental Health and School Performance: Findings from a Randomized Controlled Trial," *Mindfulness*, Vol. 8, No. 3, June 2017, pp. 1–10.

Fraser, Mark W., Maeda J. Galinsky, Paul R. Smokowski, Steven H. Day, Mary A. Terzian, Roderick A. Rose, and Shenyang Guo, "Social Information-Processing Skills Training to Promote Social Competence and Prevent Aggressive Behavior in the Third Grades," *Journal of Consulting and Clinical Psychology*, Vol. 73, No. 6, December 2005, pp. 1045–1055.

Fraser, Mark W., Jung-Sook Lee, Lawrence L. Kupper, and Steven H. Day, "A Controlled Trial of the Making Choices Program: Six-Month Follow-Up," *Research on Social Work Practice*, Vol. 21, No. 2, March 2011, pp. 165–176.

Fraser, Mark W., Aaron M. Thompson, Steven H. Day, and Rebecca J. Macy, "The Making Choices Program: Impact of Social-Emotional Skills Training on the Risk Status of Third Graders," *Elementary School Journal*, Vol. 114, March 2014, pp. 354–379.

Frey, Karin S., Miriam K. Hirschstein, Leihua Van Schoiack Edstrom, and Jennie L. Snell, "Observed Reductions in School Bullying, Nonbullying Aggression, and Destructive Bystander Behavior: A Longitudinal Evaluation," *Journal of Educational Psychology*, Vol. 101, No. 2, May 2009, pp. 466–481.

Frey, Karin S., Miriam K. Hirschstein, Jennie L. Snell, Leihua Van Schoiack Edstrom, Elizabeth P. MacKenzie, and Carole J. Broderick, "Reducing Playground Bullying and Supporting Beliefs: An Experimental Trial of the Steps to Respect Program," *Developmental Psychology*, Vol. 41, No. 3, May 2005, pp. 479–490.

Frey, Karin S., Susan Bobbitt Nolen, Leihua Van Schoiack Edstrom, and Miriam K. Hirschstein, "Effects of a School-Based Social-Emotional Competence Program: Linking Children's Goals, Attributions, and Behavior," *Journal of Applied Developmental Psychology*, Vol. 26, No. 2, April 2005, pp. 171–200.

Gottfredson, Gary D., Elizabeth M. Jones, and Thomas W. Gore, "Implementation and Evaluation of a Cognitive–Behavioral Intervention to Prevent Problem Behavior in a Disorganized School," *Prevention Science*, Vol. 3, No. 1, March 2002, pp. 43–56.

Gould, Laura Feagans, Jacinda K. Dariotis, Tamar Mendelson, and Mark T. Greenberg, "A School-Based Mindfulness Intervention for Urban Youth: Exploring Moderators of Intervention Effects," *Journal of Community Psychology*, Vol. 40, No. 8, November 2012, pp. 968–982.

Grant, Sean, Laura S. Hamilton, Stephani L. Wrabel, Celia J. Gomez, Anamarie Auger, Jennifer Tamargo, Fatih Unlu, Emilio Chavez-Herrerias, Garrett Baker, Mark Barrett, Mark Harris, and Alyssa Ramos, *Social and Emotional Learning Interventions Under the Every Student Succeeds Act: Evidence Review—Intervention Summaries*, Santa Monica, Calif.: RAND Corporation, RR-2133/1-WF, 2017.

Grant, Sean, Paul Montgomery, Sally Hopewell, Geraldine Macdonald, David Moher, and Evan Mayo-Wilson, "Developing a Reporting Guideline for Social and Psychological Intervention Trials" *Research on Social Work Practice*, Vol. 23, No. 6, November 2013, pp. 595–602.

Guo, Shenyang, Qi Wu, Paul R. Smokowski, Martica Bacallao, Caroline B. R. Evans, and Katie L. Cotter, "A Longitudinal Evaluation of the Positive Action Program in a Low-Income, Racially Diverse, Rural County: Effects on Self-Esteem, School Hassles, Aggression, and Internalizing Symptoms," *Journal of Youth and Adolescence*, Vol. 44, No. 12, December 2015, pp. 2337–2358.

Guyatt, Gordon H., Andrew D. Oxman, Gunn E. Vist, Regina Kunz, Yngve Falck-Ytter, Pablo Alonso-Coello, and Holger J. Schünemann, "GRADE: An Emerging Consensus on Rating Quality of Evidence and Strength of Recommendations," *BMJ: British Medical Journal*, Vol. 336, No. 7650, April 2008, p. 924.

Hall, Bruce W., and Tina P. Bacon, "Building a Foundation Against Violence: Impact of a School-Based Prevention Program on Elementary Students," *Journal of School Violence*, Vol. 4, No. 4, 2005, pp. 63–83.

Hanson, Thomas, Barbara Dietsch, and Hong Zheng, *Lessons in Character Impact Evaluation*, Jessup, Md.: National Center for Education Evaluation and Regional Assistance, NCEE 2012-4004, 2012.

Harlacher, Jason E., and Kenneth W. Merrell, "Social and Emotional Learning as a Universal Level of Student Support: Evaluating the Follow-Up Effect of Strong Kids on Social and Emotional Outcomes," *Journal of Applied School Psychology*, Vol. 26, No. 3, July 2010, pp. 212–229.

Hazelden Foundation, "Violence Prevention Works! Home of the Olweus Bullying Prevention Program," website, undated. As of October 23, 2017: http://www.violencepreventionworks.org/public/index.page

Heckman, James J., and Tim Kautz, *Fostering and Measuring Skills: Interventions That Improve Character and Cognition*, Cambridge, Mass.: National Bureau of Economic Research, working paper no. 7750, 2013.

Hennessey, Beth A., "Promoting Social Competence in School-Aged Children: The Effects of the Open Circle Program," *Journal of School Psychology*, Vol. 45, No. 3, June 2004, pp. 349–360.

Herman, Rebecca, Susan M. Gates, Aziza Arifkhanova, Andriy Bega, Emilio R. Chavez-Herrerias, Eugeniu Han, Mark Harris, Jennifer Tamargo, and Stephani L. Wrabel, *School Leadership Interventions Under the Every Student Succeeds Act: Evidence Review: Updated and Expanded*, Santa Monica, Calif.: RAND Corporation, RR-1550-2-WF, 2017. As of March 14, 2017:
http://www.rand.org/pubs/research_reports/RR1550-2.html

IES—*See* Institute of Education Sciences.

"Insights Intervention," website, undated. As of October 19, 2017:
http://insightsintervention.com

Institute of Education Sciences, "Funding Opportunities," webpage, undated a. As of March 13, 2017:
https://ies.ed.gov/funding/grantsearch/

———, "Regional Educational Laboratory Program," webpage, undated b. As of March 13, 2017:
https://ies.ed.gov/ncee/edlabs/

———, "What Works Clearinghouse," webpage, undated c. As of March 13, 2017:
https://ies.ed.gov/ncee/wwc/

———, "WWC Evidence Review Protocol for Character Education Interventions," September 2006. As of March 13, 2017:
https://ies.ed.gov/ncee/wwc/Docs/ReferenceResources/CharEd_protocol.pdf

———, *What Works Clearinghouse: Procedures and Standards Handbook*, Vers. 3.0, March 2014. As of October 12, 2017:
https://ies.ed.gov/ncee/wwc/Docs/referenceresources/wwc_procedures_v3_0_standards_handbook.pdf

———, "Review of Individual Studies Protocol," Vers. 3.0, April 2016. As of October 12, 2017:
https://ies.ed.gov/ncee/wwc/Docs/ReferenceResources/wwc_ris_protocol_v3.pdf

Iris Educational Media, "We Have Skills," webpage, undated. As of October 23, 2017:
https://www.irised.com/products/we-have-skills

Jenson, Jeffery M., Daniel Brisson, Kimberly A. Bender, and Anne P. Williford, "Effects of the Youth Matters Prevention Program on Patterns of Bullying and Victimization in Elementary and Middle School," *Social Work Research*, Vol. 37, No. 4, December 2013, pp. 361–372.

Jenson, Jeffery M., and William A. Dieterich, "Effects of a Skills-Based Prevention Program on Bullying and Bully Victimization Among Elementary School Children," *Prevention Science*, Vol. 8, No. 8, December 2007, pp. 285–296.

Jenson., Jeffery M., William A. Dieterich, Daniel Brisson, Kimberly A. Bender, and Anne Powell, "Preventing Childhood Bullying: Findings and Lessons from the Denver Public Schools Trial," *Research on Social Work Practice*, Vol. 20, No. 5, February 4, 2010, pp. 509–517.

Johnson, Valarie L., Patricia Simon, and Eun-Young Mun, "A Peer-Led High School Transition Program Increases Graduation Rates Among Latino Males," *Journal of Educational Research*, Vol. 107, No. 3, May 2014, pp. 186–196.

Jones, Stephanie M., Sophie P. Barnes, Rebecca Bailey, and Emily J. Doolittle, "Promoting Social and Emotional Competencies in Elementary School," *Future of Children*, Vol. 27, No. 1., Spring 2017, pp. 49–72.

Jones, Stephanie M., and Suzanne M. Bouffard, "Social and Emotional Learning in Schools from Programs to Strategies," *SRDC Social Policy Report*, Vol. 26, No. 4, 2012. As of August 3, 2016:
http://www.srcd.org/sites/default/files/documents/spr_264_final_2.pdf

Jones, Stephanie M., Joshua L. Brown, and J. Lawrence Aber, "Two-Year Impacts of a Universal School-Based Social-Emotional and Literacy Intervention: An Experiment in Translational Developmental Research," *Child Development*, Vol. 82, No. 2, March 2011, pp. 533–554.

Jones, Stephanie M., Joshua L. Brown, Wendy L. G. Hoglund, and J. Lawrence Aber, "A School-Randomized Clinical Trial of an Integrated Social-Emotional Learning and Literacy Intervention: Impacts After 1 School Year," *Journal of Consulting and Clinical Psychology*, Vol. 78, No. 6, December 2010, pp. 829–842.

Jones, Stephanie M., Katharine Brush, Rebecca Bailey, Gretchen Brion-Miesels, Joseph McIntyre, Jennifer Kahn, Bryan Nelson, and Laura Stickle, *Navigating SEL from the Inside Out*, Cambridge, Mass.: Harvard Graduate School of Education, 2017. As of October 13, 2017:
http://www.wallacefoundation.org/knowledge-center/Documents/Navigating-Social-and-Emotional-Learning-from-the-Inside-Out.pdf

Jordan Institute for Families, "Making Choices: Social Problem-Solving Skills for Children," website, undated. As of October 19, 2017:
http://ssw.unc.edu/jif/makingchoices/index.htm

Kamps, Debra, Howard Wills, Harriett Dawson-Bannister, Linda Heitzman-Powell, Esther Kottwitz, Blake Hansen, and Kandace Fleming, "Class-Wide Function-Related Intervention Teams 'CW-FIT' Efficacy Trial Outcomes," *Journal of Positive Behavior Interventions*, Vol. 17, No. 3, July 2015, pp. 134–145.

Kane, Thomas J., "Making Evidence Locally: Rethinking Education Research Under the Every Student Succeeds Act," *Education Next*, Vol. 17, No. 2, Spring 2017. As of October 11, 2017:
http://educationnext.org/
making-evidence-locally-education-research-every-student-succeeds-act/

Kendziora, Kimberly, and Nick Yoder, *When Districts Support and Integrate Social and Emotional Learning (SEL): Findings From an Ongoing Evaluation of Districtwide Implementation of SEL*, Washington, D.C.: American Institutes for Research, 2016.

Khalsa, Sat Bir S., Lynn Hickey-Schultz, Deborah Cohen, Naomi Steiner, and Stephen Cope, "Evaluation of the Mental Health Benefits of Yoga in a Secondary School: A Preliminary Randomized Controlled Trial," *The Journal of Behavioral Health Services & Research*, Vol. 39, No. 1, January 2012, pp. 80–90.

Kidron, Yael, Mark Garibaldi, Emily Anderson, and David Osher, *Lions Quest Skills for Growing: Implementation and Outcome Study in Wood County, West Virginia*, final report, Oak Brook, Ill.: American Institutes for Research, 2015.

Kisiel, Cassandra, Margaret Blaustein, Joseph Spinazzola, Caren S. Schmidt, Marla Zucker, and Bessel van der Kolk, "Evaluation of a Theater-Based Youth Violence Prevention Program for Elementary School Children," *Journal of School Violence*, Vol. 5, No. 2, June 2006, pp. 19–36.

Korn, Shira, Martin Gamboa, and Morgan Polikoff, "Just How Common Are the Standards in Common Core States?" Philadelphia, Pa.: Center on Standards, Alignment, Instruction, and Learning, November 3, 2016. As of March 16, 2017: http://c-sail.org/resources/blog/just-how-common-are-standards-common-core-states

Lakes, Kimberley D., Tracy Bryars, Swetha Sirisinahal, Nimrah Salim, Sara Arastoo, Natasha Emmerson, Daniel Kang, Lois Shim, Doug Wong, and Chang Jin Kang, "The Healthy for Life Taekwondo Pilot Study: A Preliminary Evaluation of Effects on Executive Function and BMI, Feasibility, and Acceptability," *Mental Health and Physical Activity*, Vol. 6, No. 3, October 2013, pp. 181–188.

Lash, David, and Grace Belfiore, *The MyWays Success Framework: Student Competencies for Learning, Work, and Life*, Washington, D.C.: Next Generation Learning Challenges, 2017. As of October 13, 2017: https://myways.nextgenlearning.org/report/

Lawton, Brian, Paul R. Brandon, Louis Cicchinelli, and Wendy Kekahio, *Logic Models: A Tool for Designing and Monitoring Program Evaluations*, Washington, D.C.: Institute of Educational Science, U.S. Department of Education, REL 2014-007, 2014. As of July 31, 2017: https://ies.ed.gov/ncee/edlabs/regions/pacific/pdf/REL_2014007.pdf

Leadership Program, "Conflict Resolution Model Program—VPP," webpage, undated. As of October 23, 2017: http://tlpnyc.com/our-programs/youth-development/conflict-resolution-model-program/

LeCroy, Craig Winston, "Evaluation of an Empowerment Program for Early Adolescent Girls," *Adolescence*, Vol. 39, No. 155, Fall 2004, pp. 427–441

———, "Experimental Evaluation of 'Go Grrrls' Preventive Intervention for Early Adolescent Girls," *Journal of Primary Prevention*, Vol. 25, No. 4, December 2004, pp. 457–473.

LeCroy, Craig Winston, and Janice Daley, "Go Grrls Program," website, undated. As of October 19, 2017:
http://www.public.asu.edu/~lecroy/gogrrrls/body.htm

Lee, Laurie, John Hughes, Kevin Smith, and Barbara Foorman, *An SEA Guide for Identifying Evidence-Based Interventions for School Improvement*, Tallahassee, Fla.: Florida Center for Reading Research, Florida State University, 2016.

Leff, Stephen S., Tracy Evian Waasdorp, and Brooke S. Paskewich, "The Broader Impact of Friend to Friend (F2F): Effects on Teacher-Student Relationships, Prosocial Behaviors, and Relationally and Physically Aggressive Behaviors," *Behavior Modification*, Vol. 40, No. 4, July 2016, pp. 589–610.

Leff, Stephen S., Tracy Evian Waasdorp, Brooke Paskewich, Rebecca Lakin Gullan, Abbas F. Jawad, Julie Paquette MacEvoy, Betsy E. Feinberg, and Thomas J. Power, "The Preventing Relational Aggression in Schools Everyday Program: A Preliminary Evaluation of Acceptability and Impact," *School Psychology Review*, Vol. 39, No. 4, December 2010, pp. 569–587.

Lemberger, Matthew E., James P. Selig, Hannah Bowers, and Jennifer E. Rogers, "Effects of the Student Success Skills Program on Executive Functioning Skills, Feelings of Connectedness, and Academic Achievement in a Predominantly Hispanic, Low-Income Middle School District," *Journal of Counseling & Development*, Vol. 93, No. 1, January 2015, pp. 25–37.

Lewis, Kendra M., David L. DuBois, Niloofar Bavarian, Alan Acock, Naida Silverthorn, Joseph Day, and Brian R. Flay, "Effects of Positive Action on the Emotional Health of Urban Youth: A Cluster-Randomized Trial," *Journal of Adolescent Health*, Vol. 53, No. 6, December 2013, pp. 706–711.

Lewis, Kendra M., Marc B. Schure, Niloofar Bavarian, David L. DuBois, Joseph Day, Peter Ji, Naida Silverthorn, Alan Acock, Samuel Vuchinich, and Brian R. Flay, "Problem Behavior and Urban, Low-Income Youth: A Randomized Controlled Trial of Positive Action in Chicago," *American Journal of Preventive Medicine*, Vol. 44, No. 6, June 2013, pp. 622–630.

Lewis, Kendra M., Samuel Vuchinich, Peter Ji, David L. DuBois, Alan Acock, Niloofar Bavarian, Joseph Day, Naida Silverthorn, and Brian R. Flay, "Effects of the 'Positive Action' Program on Indicators of Positive Youth Development Among Urban Youth," *Applied Developmental Science*, Vol. 20, No. 1, January 2016, pp. 16–28.

Li, Kin-Kit, Isaac Washburn, David L. DuBois, Samuel Vuchinich, Peter Ji, Vanessa Brechling, Joseph Day, Michael W. Beets, Alan C. Acock, Michael Berbaum, Frank Snyder, and Brian R. Flay, "Effects of the Positive Action Programme on Problem Behaviours in Elementary School Students: A Matched-Pair Randomised Control Trial in Chicago," *Psychology & Health*, Vol. 26, No. 2, February 2011, pp. 187–204.

Linares, L. Oriana, Nicole Rosbruch, Marcia B. Stern, Martha E. Edwards, Gillian Walker, Howard B. Abikoff, and Jose Ma J. Alvir, "Developing Cognitive-Social-Emotional Competencies to Enhance Academic Learning," *Psychology in the Schools*, Vol. 42, No. 4, 2005, pp. 405–417.

Lions Quest, "Elementary Social and Emotional Learning," webpage, 2015. As of October 23, 2017:
https://www.lions-quest.org/elementary-social-and-emotional-learning/

Loeb, Pam, Stacia Tipton, and Erin Wagner, *Social and Emotional Learning: Feedback and Communications Insights from the Field*, slide presentation, New York: Wallace Foundation, December 2016. As of July 31, 2017:
http://www.wallacefoundation.org/knowledge-center/Pages/SEL-Feedback-and-Communications-Insights-from-the-Field.aspx

Low, Sabrina, Clayton R. Cook, Keith Smolkowski, and Jodie Buntain-Ricklefs, "Promoting Social-Emotional Competence: An Evaluation of the Elementary Version of Second Step®," *Journal of School Psychology*, Vol. 53, No. 6, December 2015, pp. 463–477.

Low, Sabrina, Karin S. Frey, and Callie J. Brockman, "Gossip on the Playground: Changes Associated with Universal Intervention, Retaliation Beliefs, and Supportive Friends," *School Psychology Review*, Vol. 39, No. 4, December 2010, pp. 536–551.

Low, Sabina, and Mark Van Ryzin, "The Moderating Effects of School Climate on Bullying Prevention Efforts," *School Psychology Quarterly*, Vol. 29, No. 3, September 2014, pp. 306–319.

Ludwig, Meredith J., Andrea Boyle, and Jim Lindsay, *Review of Evidence: Arts Integration Research Through the Lens of the Every Student Succeeds Act (ESSA)*, Washington, D.C.: American Institutes for Research, 2017. As of November 28, 2017:
http://www.wallacefoundation.org/knowledge-center/Pages/ESSA-Arts-Evidence-Review-Report.aspx

Maestas, Nicole, and Sarah J. Gaillot, *An Outcome Evaluation of the Success for Kids Program*, Santa Monica, Calif.: RAND Corporation, TR-575-1-SFK, 2010. As of February 15, 2017:
http://www.rand.org/pubs/technical_reports/TR575-1.html

Mariani, Melissa, Linda Webb, Elizabeth Villares, and Greg Brigman, "Effect of Participation in Student Success Skills on Prosocial and Bullying Behavior," *Professional Counselor*, Vol. 5, No. 3, 2015, pp. 341–353.

Marquez, Brion, Jessie Marquez, Claudia G. Vincent, Jordan Pennefather, Jeffery R. Sprague, Keith Smolkowski, and Pamela Yeaton, "The Iterative Development and Initial Evaluation of We Have Skills! An Innovative Approach to Teaching Social Skills to Elementary Students," *Education and Treatment of Children*, Vol. 37, No. 1, February 2014, pp. 137–161.

Mathematica Policy Research, "RCT-YES," website, 2016. As of July 31, 2017: https://www.rct-yes.com/

Mauricio, Anne M., Francesca Dillman-Carpentier, and John Horan, "An Experimental Evaluation of an Internet-Delivered Conflict Resolution Skills Curriculum in a Secondary School Setting," *Journal of School Violence*, Vol. 4, No. 3, October 2005, pp. 37–48.

McClowry, Sandra, David L. Snow, and Catherine S. Tamis-LeMonda, "An Evaluation of the Effects of 'INSIGHTS' on the Behavior of Inner City Primary School Children," *Journal of Primary Prevention*, Vol. 26, No. 6, November 2005, pp. 567–584.

McCormick, Meghan P., Elise Cappella, Erin E. O'Connor, Jennifer L. Hill and Sandee G. McClowry, "Do Effects of Social- Emotional Learning Programs Vary by Level of Parent Participation? Evidence from the Randomized Trial of INSIGHTS," *Journal of Research on Educational Effectiveness*, Vol. 9, No. 3, 2016, pp. 364–394.

McCormick, Meghan P., Elise Cappella, Erin E. O'Connor, and Sandee G. McClowry, "Context Matters for Social-Emotional Learning: Examining Variation in Program Impact by Dimensions of School Climate," *American Journal of Community Psychology*, Vol. 56, No. 1–2, September 2015, pp. 101–119.

Melnick, Hanna, Channa Cook-Harvey, and Linda Darling-Hammond, *Encouraging Social and Emotional Learning in the Context of New Accountability*, Palo Alto, Calif.: Learning Policy Institute, April 18, 2017. As of October 26, 2017:
https://learningpolicyinstitute.org/product/encouraging-social-emotional-learning-new-accountability-report

Menard, Scott, and Jennifer K. Grotpeter, "Evaluation of Bully-Proofing Your School as an Elementary School Antibullying Intervention," *Journal of School Violence*, Vol. 13, No. 2, 2014, pp. 188–209.

Menard, Scott, Jennifer Grotpeter, Danielle Gianola, and Maura O'Neal, *Evaluation of Bully-Proofing Your School: Final Report*, Washington, D.C.: National Institute of Justice, Office of Justice Programs, Office of Juvenile Justice and Delinquency Prevention, 2008.

Mendelson, Tamar, Mark T. Greenberg, Jacinda K. Dariotis, Laura F Gould, Brittany L. Rhoades, and Philip J. Leaf, "Feasibility and Preliminary Outcomes of a School-Based Mindfulness Intervention for Urban Youth," *Journal of Abnormal Child Psychology*, Vol. 38, No. 7, October 2010, pp. 985–994.

Mendelson, Tamar, S. Darius Tandon, Lindsey O'Brennan, Philip J. Leaf, and Nicholas S. Ialongo, "Moving Prevention into Schools: The Impact of a Trauma-Informed School-Based Intervention," *Journal of Adolescence*, Vol. 43, August 2015, pp. 142–147.

Mendez Foundation, "Too Good: Prevention Education Through Social and Emotional Learning," website, undated. As of October 23, 2017:
http://www.toogoodprograms.org/

Michigan Department of Health and Human Services, "Michigan Model for Health Grades K-12," webpage, undated. As of October 23, 2017:
http://www.michigan.gov/mdhhs/0,5885,7-339-73971_4911_4912_74286---,00.html

Morningside Center for Teaching Social Responsibility, "The 4Rs Program," webpage, undated a. As of October 19, 2017:
http://www.morningsidecenter.org/4rs-program

———, "Resolving Conflict Creatively Program," webpage, undated b. As of October 23, 2017:
http://www.morningsidecenter.org/resolving-conflict-creatively-program

Nagaoka, Jenny, Camille A. Farrington, Stacy B. Ehrlich, Ryan D. Heath, David W. Johnson, Sarah Dickson, Ashley C. Turner, Ashley Mayo, and Kathleen Hayes, *Foundations for Young Adult Success: A Developmental Framework*, Chicago, Ill.: Consortium on Chicago School Research, 2015.

Napoli, Maria, Paul Rock Krech, and Lynn C. Holley, "Mindfulness Training for Elementary School Students: The Attention Academy," *Journal of Applied School Psychology*, Vol. 21, No. 1, July 2005, pp. 99–125.

National Academies of Sciences, Engineering, and Medicine, *Supporting Students' College Success: Assessment of Intrapersonal and Interpersonal Competencies. Board on Testing and Assessment, Division of Behavioral and Social Sciences and Education*, Washington, D.C.: National Academies Press, 2016.

National Center for School Engagement, "Bully-Proofing Your School," webpage, undated. As of October 19, 2017:
http://schoolengagement.org/school-engagement-services/bully-proofing-your-school/

National Research Council, *Education for Life and Work: Developing Transferable Knowledge and Skills in the 21st Century*, Washington, D.C.: National Academies Press, 2012.

Neace, William P., and Marco A. Munoz, "Pushing the Boundaries of Education: Evaluating the "Impact of Second Step®—A Violence Prevention Curriculum" with Psychosocial and Non-Cognitive Measures," *Child & Youth Services*, Vol. 33, No. 1, January 2012, pp. 46–69.

Noggle, Jessica J., Naomi J. Steiner, Takuya Minami, and Sat Bir S. Khalsa, "Benefits of Yoga for Psychosocial Well-Being in a US High School Curriculum: A Preliminary Randomized Controlled Trial," *Journal of Developmental and Behavioral Pediatrics*, Vol. 33, No. 3, April 2012, pp. 193–201.

NRC—*See* National Research Council.

O'Connor, Erin E., Elise Cappella, Meghan P. McCormick, and Sandee G. McClowry, "Enhancing the Academic Development of Shy Children: A Test of the Efficacy of INSIGHTS," *School Psychology Review*, Vol. 43, No. 3, September 2014a, pp. 239–259.

———, "An Examination of the Efficacy of Insights in Enhancing the Academic and Behavioral Development of Children in Early Grades," *Journal of Educational Psychology*, Vol. 106, No. 4, November 2014b, pp. 1156–1169.

O'Connor, Rosemarie, Jessica De Feyter, Alyssa Carr, Jia Lisa Luo, and Helen Romm, *A Review of the Literature on Social and Emotional Learning for Students Ages 3–8: Characteristics of Effective Social and Emotional Learning Programs (Part 1 of 4)*, Washington, D.C.: U.S. Department of Education, Institute of Education Sciences, National Center for Education Evaluation and Regional Assistance, Regional Educational Laboratory Mid-Atlantic, 2017.

O'Hearn, Todd C., and Margaret Gatz, "Going for the Goal: Improving Youths' Problem-Solving Skills Through a School-Based Intervention," *Journal of Community Psychology*, Vol. 30, No. 3, May 2002, pp. 281–303.

O'Neill, James M., Jeffrey K. Clark, and James A. Jones, "Promoting Mental Health and Preventing Substance Abuse and Violence in Elementary Students: A Randomized Control Study of the Michigan Model for Health," *Journal of School Health*, Vol. 81, No. 6, June 2011, pp. 320–330.

Oregon Resiliency Project, "Strong Kids," website, undated. As of October 23, 2017:
http://strongkids.uoregon.edu/strongkids.html

Osher, David, Yael Kidron, Marc Brackett, Allison Dymnicki, Stephanie Jones, and Roger P. Weissberg, "Advancing the Science and Practice of Social and Emotional Learning: Looking Back and Moving Forward," *Review of Research in Education*, Vol. 40, No. 1, December 2016, pp. 644–681.

Ottmar, Erin R., Sara E. Rimm-Kaufman, Ross A. Larsen, and Robert Q. Berry, "Mathematical Knowledge for Teaching, Standards-Based Mathematics Teaching Practices, and Student Achievement in the Context of the Responsive Classroom Approach," *American Educational Research Journal*, Vol. 52, No. 4, 2015, pp. 787–821.

Oyserman, Daphna, Deborah Bybee, and Kathy Terry, "Possible Selves and Academic Outcomes: How and When Possible Selves Impel Action," *Journal of Personality and Social Psychology*, Vol. 91, No. 1, July 2006, pp. 188–204.

Page, B., and A. D'Agostino, *Connect with Kids: 2004–2005 Study Results for Kansas and Missouri*, Durham, N.C.: Compass Consulting Group, LLC, 2005.

PATHS Training, homepage, 2012. As of October 23, 2017:
http://www.pathstraining.com/main/

Paxis International, "PAX Good Behavior Game," website, undated. As of October 19, 2017:
http://goodbehaviorgame.org

Pearson's Clinical Assessment Group, "Social Skills Improvement Overview," webpage, undated. As of October 23, 2017:
https://www.pearsonclinical.com/education/RelatedInfo/ssis-overview.html

Petticrew, Mark, and Helen Roberts, *Systematic Reviews in the Social Sciences: A Practical Guide*, Oxford, UK: Blackwell Publishing, 2008.

Playworks, homepage, undated. As of October 23, 2017:
http://www.playworks.org/

Polanin, Joshua R., and Dorothy L. Espelage, "Using a Meta-Analytic Technique to Assess the Relationship Between Treatment Intensity and Program Effects in a Cluster-Randomized Trial," *Journal of Behavioral Education*, Vol. 24, No. 1, March 2015, pp. 133–151.

Positive Action, homepage, undated. As of October 23, 2017:
https://www.positiveaction.net/

Public Law 107-279, Education Sciences Reform Act of 2002, January 23, 2002.

Public Law 114-95, Every Student Succeeds Act, December 10, 2015.

Quach, Dianna, Kristen E. Jastrowski Mano, and Kristi Alexander, "A Randomized Controlled Trial Examining the Effect of Mindfulness Meditation on Working Memory Capacity in Adolescents," *Journal of Adolescent Health*, Vol. 58, No. 5, May 2016, pp. 489–496.

REL Pacific, "ELM Application," webpage, undated. As of October 12, 2017:
http://relpacific.mcrel.org/resources/elm-app/

Renshaw, Tyler L., and Shane R. Jimerson, "Enhancing Student Attitudes via a Brief, Universal-Level Bullying Prevention Curriculum," *School Mental Health*, Vol. 4, No. 2, June 2012, pp. 115–128.

Responsive Classroom, homepage, undated. As of October 23, 2017:
https://www.responsiveclassroom.org/

Results for America, "Helping Education Leaders Build and Use Evidence to Improve Student Outcomes," webpage, undated. As of October 11, 2017: http://results4america.org/our-work/evidence-in-education-lab/

———, *Leverage Points: Thirteen Opportunities for State Education Agencies to Use Their ESSA State Plans to Build and Use Evidence to Improve Student Outcomes*, Washington, D.C., 2017.

Riggs, Nathaniel R., Mark T. Greenberg, Carol A. Kusché, and Mary Ann Pentz, "The Mediational Role of Neurocognition in the Behavioral Outcomes of a Social-Emotional Prevention Program in Elementary School Students: Effects of the PATHS Curriculum," *Prevention Science*, Vol. 7, No. 1, March 2006, pp. 91–102.

Rimm-Kaufman, Sara E., and Yu-Jen I. Chiu, "Promoting Social and Academic Competence in the Classroom: An Intervention Study Examining the Contribution of the Responsive Classroom Approach," *Psychology in the Schools*, Vol. 44, No. 4, April 2007, pp. 397–413.

Rimm-Kaufman, Sara E., Xitao Fan, Yu-Jen Chiu, and Wenyi You, "The Contribution of the Responsive Classroom Approach on Children's Academic Achievement: Results from a Three Year Longitudinal Study," *Journal of School Psychology*, Vol. 45, No. 4, August 2007, pp. 401–421.

Rimm-Kaufman, Sara E., Ross A. Larsen, Alison E. Baroody, Timothy W. Curby, Michelle Ko, Julia B. Thomas, Eileen G. Merritt, Tashia Abry, and Jamie DeCoster, "Efficacy of the Responsive Classroom Approach: Results from a 3-Year, Longitudinal Randomized Controlled Trial," *American Educational Research Journal*, Vol. 51, No. 3, June 2014, pp. 567–603.

Roberts, Laura, Peter Yeomans, and Susan Ferro-Almeida, "Project WIN Evaluation Shows Decreased Violence and Improved Conflict Resolution Skills for Middle School Students," *RMLE Online: Research in Middle Level Education*, Vol. 30, No. 8, January 2007, pp. 1–14.

Rutgers University, "Talking with TJ," website, undated. As of October 23, 2017: http://www.rci.rutgers.edu/~melias/tj.html

Schonfeld, David J., Ryan E. Adams, Bridget K. Fredstrom, Roger P. Weissberg, Richard Gilman, Charlene Voyce, Ricarda Tomlin, and Dee Speese-Linehan, "Cluster-Randomized Trial Demonstrating Impact on Academic Achievement of Elementary Social-Emotional Learning," *School Psychology Quarterly*, Vol. 30, No. 3, September 2015, pp. 406–420.

Shakman, Karen, "Logic Models to Support Program Design, Implementation and Evaluation: A Workbook Created by the REgional Educational Laboratory–Northeast and Islands," for the ISBE 21st CCLC Program Evaluation Webinar, April 15, 2014. As of July 31, 2017:
http://www.sedl.org/afterschool/iqa/events/webinars/LogicModel_Workbook_2014.pdf

Shakman, Karen, and Sheila M. Rodriguez, *Logic Models for Program Design, Implementation, and Evaluation: Workshop Toolkit*, Institute of Education Sciences, National Center for Education Evaluation and Regional Assistance, May 2015. As of July 31, 2017:
https://ies.ed.gov/ncee/edlabs/regions/northeast/pdf/REL_2015057.pdf

Shapiro, Jeremy P., Joella D. Burgoon, Carolyn J. Welker, and Joseph B. Clough, "Evaluation of the Peacemakers Program: School-Based Violence Prevention for Students in Grades Four Through Eight," *Psychology in the Schools*, Vol. 39, No. 1, January 2002, pp. 87–100.

Sibinga, Erica M. S., Lindsey Webb, Sharon R. Ghazarian, and Jonathan M. Ellen, "School-Based Mindfulness Instruction: An RCT," *Pediatrics*, Vol. 137, No. 1, January 2016, p. e20152532.

Slavin, Robert, and Elizabeth Kim, "Reviewing Social and Emotional Learning for ESSA: MOOSES, not Parrots," *HuffPost Blog*, May 25, 2017. As of July 3, 2017:
http://www.huffingtonpost.com/entry/reviewing-social-and-emotional-learning-for-essa-mooses_us_591d9505e4b07617ae4cb9a0

Smith, Charles, Gina McGovern, Reed Larson, Barbara Hillaker, and Stephen C. Peck, *Preparing Youth to Thrive: Promising Practices for Social Emotional Learning*, Washington, D.C.: Forum for Youth Investment, 2016.

Smith, Stephen W., Ann P. Daunic, Burak Aydin, Christopher L. Van Loan, and Gregory G. Taylor, "Effect of Tools for Getting Along on Student Risk for Emotional and Behavioral Problems in Upper Elementary Classrooms: A Replication Study," *School Psychology Review*, Vol. 45, No. 1, March 2016, pp. 73–92.

Smith, Stephen W., Ann P. Daunic, Brian R. Barber, Burak Aydin, Christopher L. Van Loan, and Gregory G. Taylor, "Preventing Risk for Significant Behavior Problems Through a Cognitive-Behavioral Intervention: Effects of the Tools for Getting Along Curriculum at One-Year Follow-Up," *Journal of Primary Prevention*, Vol. 35, No. 5, October 2014, pp. 371–387.

Smokowski, Paul R., Mark W. Fraser, Steven H. Day, Maeda J. Galinsky, and Marticia L. Bacallao, "School-Based Skills Training to Prevent Aggressive Behavior and Peer Rejection in Childhood: Evaluating the Making Choices Program," *Journal of Primary Prevention*, Vol. 25, No. 2, October 2004, pp. 233–251.

Smokowski, Paul R., Shenyang Guo, Qi Wu, Caroline B. R. Evans, Katie L. Cotter, and Marticia L. Bacallao, "Evaluating Dosage Effects for the Positive Action Program: How Implementation Impacts Internalizing Symptoms, Aggression, School Hassles, and Self-Esteem," *American Journal of Orthopsychiatry*, Vol. 86, No. 3, 2016, pp. 310–322.

Snyder, Frank J., Alan C. Acock, Samuel Vuchinich, Michael W. Beets, Isaac J. Washburn, and Brian R. Flay, "Preventing Negative Behaviors Among Elementary-School Students Through Enhancing Students' Social-Emotional and Character Development," *American Journal of Health Promotion*, Vol. 28, No. 1, September 2013, pp. 50–58.

Snyder, Frank, Brian Flay, Samuel Vuchinich, Alan Acock, Isaac Washburn, Michael Beets, and Kin-Kit Li, "Impact of a Social-Emotional and Character Development Program on School-Level Indicators of Academic Achievement, Absenteeism, and Disciplinary Outcomes: A Matched-Pair, Cluster-Randomized, Controlled Trial," *Journal of Research on Educational Effectiveness*, Vol. 3, No. 1, December 2010, pp. 26–55.

Snyder, Frank J., Samuel Vuchinich, Alan Acock, Isaac J. Washburn, and Brian R. Flay, "Improving Elementary School Quality Through the Use of a Social-Emotional and Character Development Program: A Matched-Pair, Cluster-Randomized, Controlled Trial in Hawai'i," *Journal of School Health*, Vol. 82, No. 1, January 2012, pp. 11–20.

Soland, Jim, Laura S. Hamilton, and Brian M. Stecher, *Measuring 21st-Century Competencies: Guidance for Educators*, New York: Asia Society, 2013.

Song, Mengli, and Rebecca Herman, *A Practical Guide on Designing and Conducting Impact Studies in Education: Lessons Learned from the What Works Clearinghouse (Phase I)*, Washington, D.C.: American Institutes for Research, 2009. As of July 31, 2017:
http://www.air.org/sites/default/files/downloads/report/Song__Herman_WWC_Lessons_Learned_2010_0.pdf

Spirituality for Kids International Inc., "SFK.org," website, undated. As of October 23, 2017:
https://sfk.org/

Stecher, Brian M., and Laura S. Hamilton, *Measuring Hard-to-Measure Student Competencies: A Research and Development Plan*, Santa Monica, Calif.: RAND Corporation, RR-863-WFHF, 2014. As of February 15, 2017:
http://www.rand.org/pubs/research_reports/RR863.html

Stevahn, Laurie, David W. Johnson, Roger T. Johnson, and Ray Schultz, "Effects of Conflict Resolution Training Integrated into a High School Social Studies Curriculum," *Journal of Social Psychology*, Vol. 142, No. 3, June 2002, pp. 305–331.

Student Success Skills, homepage, undated. As of October 23, 2017: http://studentsuccessskills.com/

Taylor, Rebecca D., Eva Oberle, Joseph A. Durlak, and Roger P. Weissberg, "Promoting Positive Youth Development Through School-Based Social and Emotional Learning Interventions: A Meta-Analysis of Follow-Up Effects," *Child Development*, Vol. 88, No. 4, 2017, pp. 1156–1171.

Terzian, Mary A., Jilan Li, Mark W. Fraser, Steven H. Day, and Roderick A. Rose, "Social Information–Processing Skills and Aggression: A Quasi-Experimental Trial of the Making Choices and Making Choices Plus Programs," *Research on Social Work Practice*, Vol. 25, No. 3, 2015, pp. 358–369.

Thompkins, Amanda C., Lisa M. Chauveron, Ofer Harel, and Daniel F. Perkins, "Optimizing Violence Prevention Programs: An Examination of Program Effectiveness Among Urban High School Students," *Journal of School Health*, Vol. 84, No. 7, July 2014, pp. 435–443.

"Tools of the Mind," homepage, undated. As of October 23, 2017: http://toolsofthemind.org/

Torgerson, Carole J., and David J. Torgerson, "The Need for Randomised Controlled Trials in Educational Research," *British Journal of Educational Studies*, Vol. 49, No. 3, September 2001, pp. 316–328.

Transforming Education, "Measuring MESH: Student and Teacher Surveys Curated for the CORE Districts," Boston, April 2016. As of August 7, 2017: https://www.transformingeducation.org/measuring-mesh/

University of Florida, College of Education, "Tools for Getting Along," website, undated. As of October 23, 2017: https://education.ufl.edu/behavior-management-resource-guide/tools-for-getting-along-curriculum/

University of Washington, Social Development Research Group, "Raising Health Children," webpage, undated. As of October 23, 2017: http://www.sdrg.org/rhcsummary.asp

University of Wisconsin–Extension, "Program Development and Evaluation," website, September 16, 2016. As of July 31, 2017: http://fyi.uwex.edu/programdevelopment/

"Urban Improv," homepage, undated. As of October 23, 2017: http://urbanimprov.org/

U.S. Department of Education, homepage, undated. As of July 31, 2017: https://www.ed.gov/

———, *Non-Regulatory Guidance: Using Evidence to Strengthen Education Investments*, Washington, D.C., September 16, 2016.

———, "Definitions and Selection Criteria That Apply to Direct Grant Programs," July 31, 2017. As of October 12, 2017: https://www.federalregister.gov/documents/2017/07/31/2017-15989/definitions-and-selection-criteria-that-apply-to-direct-grant-programs

Wang, Cixin, Lauren Couch, Geovanna Rosas Rodriguez, and Catherine Lee, "The Bullying Literature Project: Using Children's Literature to Promote Prosocial Behavior and Social-Emotional Outcomes Among Elementary School Students," *Contemporary School Psychology*, Vol. 19, No. 4, 2015, pp. 320–329.

Weis, Robert, Karen J. Osborne, and Emily L. Dean, “Effectiveness of a Universal, Interdependent Group Contingency Program on Children’s Academic Achievement: A Countywide Evaluation,” *Journal of Applied School Psychology*, Vol. 31, No. 3, July 2015, pp. 199–218.

Wellesley Centers for Women, “Open Circle,” website, undated. As of October 23, 2017:
https://www.open-circle.org/

Wendt, Staci, Jerry Hipps, Allan Abrams, Jamie Grant, Laurent Valosek, and Sanford Nidich, “Practicing Transcendental Meditation in High Schools: Relationship to Well-Being and Academic Achievement Among Students,” *Contemporary School Psychology*, Vol. 19, No. 4, December 2015, pp. 312–319.

West, Martin R., “Framing Remarks,” in Marty West, Carrie Conaway, Russell Johnston, Venessa Keesler, Karen Ruple, Nate Schwartz, and Rita Fentress, *ESSA and Research Evidence: Opportunities and Challenges for States*, slides from presentations to the American Youth Policy Forum webinar, March 7, 2017. As of March 13, 2017:
http://www.aypf.org/wp-content/uploads/2017/03/3.7-Master-Deck.pdf

White, Laura Santangelo, “Reducing Stress in School-Age Girls Through Mindful Yoga,” *Journal of Pediatric Health Care*, Vol. 26, No. 1, February 2012, pp. 45–56.

W.K. Kellogg Foundation, “W.K. Kellogg Foundation Logic Model Development Guide,” February 2, 2006. As of October 12, 2017:
https://www.wkkf.org/resource-directory/resource/2006/02/wk-kellogg-foundation-logic-model-development-guide

Yale Center for Emotional Intelligence, “RULER” website, 2013. As of October 23, 2017:
http://ei.yale.edu/ruler/ruler-overview/

Yeager, David S., “Social-Emotional Learning Programs for Adolescents,” *The Future of Children*, Vol. 27, No. 1, Spring 2017, pp. 73–94.